Sign Me Up!

Sign Me Up!

A Marketer's Guide to Creating Email Newsletters That Build Relationships and Boost Sales

by Matt Blumberg & Michael Mayor
with Tami Monahan Forman & Stephanie A. Miller

A Return Path Book

iUniverse, Inc.
New York Lincoln Shanghai

Sign Me Up!
A Marketer's Guide to Creating Email Newsletters
That Build Relationships and Boost Sales

iUniverse books may be ordered through booksellers or by contacting:

iUniverse
2021 Pine Lake Road, Suite 100
Lincoln, NE 68512
www.iuniverse.com
1-800-Authors (1-800-288-4677)

ISBN: 0-595-33586-1 (Pbk)
ISBN: 0-595-66975-1 (Cloth)

Printed in the United States of America

To the clients of Return Path and NetCreations, who work tirelessly to make online marketing better and more successful, one email at a time.

Contents

Acknowledgements

The four of us listed on the cover of this book are but the tip of a very large iceberg. This book simply would not have been possible without the contributions of many smart people. So we would like to thank all of you listed here for your generosity and assistance in the development and creation of this book.

First, we owe a huge debt of gratitude to the employees of Return Path, each of whom is dedicated to making email work better for consumers and businesses. Eternal thanks and gratitude to:

Anita Absey, Robert Barclay, Gaetano Bavaro, Dan Breggin, Amber Brown, Carly Brantz, Julie Buchanan, Tyler Buhl, Paul Buster, Diz Carter, Joe Carvalho, Henry Chau, Jeremy Dean, Anthony DeAngelis, John DeFilippis, Kevin Delaney, Jeff Derby, Dan Diekhoff, Justin Fisk, Karl Florida, Mark Galliher, Stacy Goldin, Jeremy Goldsmith, Kirk Henry, Alex Kasiansky, Julia Khavich, Laura LaLuna, Eunhee Lee, Paul Leibrock, Allen Louie, Nathan Lynch, Patty Mah, Chad Malchow, Jonathan Mark, Jeff Mattes, Robert Mattes, Pavel Maximov, Jeremy McGuire, Whitney McNamara, Sophie Miller, Alyssa Nahatis, Kevin Noonan, Amy Norton, Rebecca Premus, Leslie Price, Mukta Rane, Kendall Rawls, Amy Reilly, Julien Ruaux, Tom Sather, Andy Sautins, Tammy Shimp, David Sieh, Jack Sinclair, Tim Skennion, Jim Smith, Carrie Spafford, John Taliercio, Edward Taussig, Jonathan Tice, Ninon Traugott, Elizabeth Vasquez, Tom Walsh, Adam Weinstein, Brian Westnedge, Jennifer Wilson, Ranee Wilson and David Zipkin

We would like to give special acknowledgement to our deliverability gurus, George Bilbrey, Tom Bartel and Leslie Price, for their expertise and patient willingness to share it!

We'd also like to thank all Return Path alumni for the role they've played in our company's development over the past five years (with sincere apologies to anyone we may have inadvertently neglected):

Tom Burke, Doug Campbell, Rory Carr, Lisa Carrieri, Edwin Castillo, Neil Cohen, Aaron Couts, Melanie Danchisko, John Darrah, James Dezendorf, Michael Doherty, Tim Dolan, Beth Feresten, Jacob Fink, Steve Gorman, Scott Green, Suzanne Halbeisen, Randolph Hernandez, Alexis Katzowitz, Brendon Kearney, Austin Kenny, Kevin King, Julia Knowlton, Kate Kuckro, Elsa Kuo, Amy Leymaster, John Mathew, Topher McGibbon, Mary Lynn McGrath, Mike Mearls, Rachel Moore, Alison Murdock, Nick Nicholas, Kevin O'Connell, Dave Paulus, Alice Pham, Jon Pierce, Linda Ryan, Jennifer Roller, Vince Sabio, Dave Smith, Stacey Smith, Matt Spielman, Remy Taylor, Walter Thames, Rebecca Thomas, John Ventura, Chris Wade, Brent Wagner, Andrew Wilson and Michael Zhang

A picture may be worth a thousand words, but we only need one to show our appreciation to Kevin Menzie of Slice of Lime for providing graphics that illustrate key concepts throughout the book: Thanks!

Thanks also go to consultants Andy Sernovitz and Rich Mintzer, who provided assistance in the early stages of this project.

We wouldn't be in a position to write this book were it not for the ongoing support of our investors and board members (both present and past). Fred Wilson, Greg Sands, Brad Feld, Chris Wand, Jonathan Shapiro, Eric Kirby, Ben Perez, Phil Summe, Chris Hoerenz, James Marciano and a host of friends and family angel investors have worked tirelessly on our behalf and written many checks along the way these past five years.

In addition, we want to thank the following smart marketers for offering examples, quotes, screen shots, advice and more. This book would not be nearly as rich without their invaluable contributions.

Jordan Ayan, SubscriberMail
Angela Caltagirone, Williams-Sonoma Inc.
Beth Fisher, American Management Association
Timothy Foy, Lenox
Gretchen Harding, BabyCenter
Anne Holland, MarketingSherpa
Monica Hoyer, iVillage
Mark Hurst, Good Experience
Chris Kilbourne, Business & Legal Reports

Melissa Lederer, CoolSavings
Mary Liao, DotGlu
Mary K. Marsden, Message Effect, Inc.
Chris Michel, Military.com
Kristin Miller, Kimberly Clark Professional
Eliot Pierce, New York Times Digital
Brian Pozesky, CoolSavings
Meg Reynolds, REI
Kathy Ruggiero, EasyAsk
Pete Sheinbaum, DailyCandy

Last, but certainly not least, a huge, huge thanks to our editor, John Renz from AdGuy Copywriting & Creative Services, for his invaluable work in turning a lot of good ideas into a cohesive book. John, we thank you for keeping us on schedule, for providing your insights and honesty and for keeping your sense of humor (and reminding us to keep our own!) throughout this project.

Thank you for your support

For each book sold, 10% of the purchase price will be donated to The Accelerated Cure Project for Multiple Sclerosis, a national nonprofit dedicated to curing Multiple Sclerosis (MS) by determining its causes. Learn more about them by visiting www.acceleratedcure.org. This cause is important personally to each of us at Return Path and we dedicate these contributions to our friend and colleague Sophie Miller, in gratitude for all she has taught us about hope, strength, faith and courage.

Preface

We love email. We were relatively early adopters of it for personal use, with accounts at places like Pipeline, Prodigy, Delphi and Compuserve—companies that seem distant and almost nostalgic here in 2004. We started working with email as a commercial messaging platform as early as 1995. Needless to say, we're quite familiar with its potential as a marketing vehicle.

What we've come to realize is that Americans have long operated under an unwritten arrangement with media companies that we call the "Old Media Deal." The Old Media Deal is simple: we say we don't like advertising, but we are willing to put up with an amazing amount of it in exchange for free or cheap content. We list a number of examples in the first chapter. The bottom line is this: advertising doesn't bug us if it's not too intrusive and if there's something in it for us.

With the advent of the internet and email, we've recognized that there's a significantly different "New Media Deal" in the works. The New Media deal is that we are willing to share a certain amount of personal information in exchange for even better content, more personalized services, or even more targeted marketing—again, as long as those things aren't too intrusive and provide adequate value. Think about how the New Media Deal works:

- We tell Yahoo! that we like the Yankees and that we own MSFT stock in order to get a personalized homepage
- We tell the *New York Times* our annual income in order to get the entire newspaper online for free
- We let Google scan our emails to put ads in them based on the content to get a free email account
- We give our email address out to receive marketing offers (even in this day and age of spam) by the millions every day

After a few years of talking somewhat circuitously about this New Media Deal, we recently found some research that backs up the theory. In a study conducted by ChoiceStream in May 2004, 81% of internet users expressed a desire for personalized content, 64% said they'd provide insight into their preferences in exchange for personalized product and content recommendations, 56% would provide demographic data for the same and 40% said they'd even agree to more comprehensive clickstream and transaction monitoring. All of these responses were stronger among younger users but healthy among all users. Sounds like a New Media Deal to us—not to mention a great opportunity for marketers.

Don't get us wrong—we still think there's a time and a place for anonymity, and it's good that we have privacy advocates who are vigilant about potential and actual abuses of data collection. But it's becoming increasingly clear that we have a New Media Deal with consumers when we send them email. The deal is this: people are willing to sacrifice their anonymity and give up their personal information in a heartbeat if the value exchange is there.

We are building Return Path's email services businesses to do just that—help clients provide value as their part of the New Media Deal. We've done that because we think it's the right thing to do, and also because it's good business. Treating the consumer not just fairly and properly but as a valued member of your company's community produces better short-term value (sales) and better long-term value (branding) for any business. These are our principles and our guiding themes behind the advice we provide to marketers and publishers in this book.

Thank you for picking up and hopefully reading this book. We look forward to your comments and ideas.

Matt Blumberg
Michael Mayor
Tami Monahan Forman
Stephanie A. Miller
New York, NY
October 2004

Introduction

The World Is Waiting for Your Email

Used properly, email can be one of the most powerful and influential forms of marketing media available. If you approach it ethically and intelligently, people will gladly give you their names, email addresses, and other valuable demographic information. They will practically roll out a red carpet to their inbox for you. They will enthusiastically sign up to receive your marketing messages!

Regretfully, far too many marketers (not spammers, mind you, but legitimate marketers with major international brands and tremendous resources at their disposal) send shoddy, poorly conceived and even crass email messages that do little more than irritate the people who are unfortunate enough to receive them. These emails are a waste of time and effort and only succeed at creating a negative stereotype for all who market via email.

However, one fact remains consistently indisputable: the most successful and profitable email marketers have built their business—and their good reputations—by providing the type of value and interest that can only be generated by implementing an email newsletter program.

These marketers have all figured out exactly what a good email newsletter program can do, which is

- Attract new customers
- Boost customer satisfaction and loyalty
- Increase response
- Self-segment your audience

Great Email Is within Your Grasp

The purpose of this book is to help you achieve all of these goals through an effective email newsletter program. We will reveal the secret ingredients necessary to create, launch and sustain an email newsletter campaign so that you too will know how to do the following:

1

- Develop a winning content strategy
- Build your brand
- Grow your business
- Connect with customers and prospects
- Build a large and responsive subscriber base
- Optimize your email newsletter program using simple yet effective techniques to track results, analyze metrics and monitor deliverability

We've divided this book into three parts, each of which covers a critical aspect of the email newsletter process.

Part I: Content Strategies—Uncover all of the aspects of a good email newsletter, and learn how to write and design one of your own.

Part II: List Strategies—Discover how to build and maintain a responsive list of your business's most appropriate audiences.

Part III: Optimization Strategies—Understand how to improve response and build relationships with your marketplace, and measure how well your email newsletter program is working.

Lessons from the Inbox:
THE RULES

We know you're itching to get started, but before we do, let's get a few things straight. There are several "pay-to-play" rules that form the foundation of all good, ethical email marketing initiatives. If you can't follow them, the rest of this book will be a waste of your time. But consider this: if you don't follow these rules, then it's a pretty good bet that your email marketing efforts will be a waste of your audience's time. And that's not good for them or for your business.

Rule #1: Don't Spam

You should not, under any circumstances, send email to people without their permission. That's "spam," the most insulting, dirty and disgusting descriptor in the email business. If this was the Wild West, calling someone a "spammer" would be fightin' words. It's unwanted and can totally discredit your business. Worse yet, it's illegal. That's right—*illegal*. There is new federal legislation that allows spammers to be prosecuted. In other words, if you send spam, you could go to jail! Learn more about these laws in Chapter 9.

The only legitimate means of email marketing is by permission. So, the number one rule in email marketing is this: Never send an email without the permission of the person receiving it.

Rule #2: Don't Send Horrible Email:

Horrible email is everywhere. Poorly conceived. Not targeted. Hard to read. Not requested. Unfortunately, because email marketing is seen as cheap and fast, it can be tempting to spend less time and pay less attention to the email campaign than you would on other more costly efforts, like direct mail. Resist the urge to treat email as less important, and thus less in need of time and effort, than your other marketing efforts. Every email that you send should be well designed, well written, engaging and relevant to the recipient. The rewards of doing so will be worth the effort.

Rule #3: Don't Hold Your Audience Hostage

Every email address you collect is precious and should be treated as such. However, if folks no longer want to be on your list, you must let them go. Remember Rule #1: it's never okay to send email to people who don't want it. That includes people who gave you permission but now want to withdraw it. If you do not follow this rule, you risk destroying your relationship with that customer forever. Ad agency Quris found that 45% of respondents in a survey said that they had stopped doing business with a company because of bad email practices.

Rule #4: Create Email That People Love to Read

Content is king: If recipients don't read your email, it has no chance of building your business, and no one will read it unless the content is relevant and interesting to them. Therefore, only create email that has real value to your audience. Figure out what they want from you and give it to them. Be relentless advocates for the reader. Stay true to the needs and wants of your subscribers—who are, after all, your customers—and they will look forward to getting your emails.

PART I

Content Strategies

This section can be summed up in three words: relevance, relevance, relevance.

Email newsletters (and your email program, for that matter) will have absolutely no impact if they're not relevant. They also need to be well written and properly designed, but that should go without saying. And, as with most marketing activities, it doesn't really cost more money to send quality email than it costs to send junk email. It may take a little more time and a couple of extra dollars, but if you want a response, this is what's required.

Think about it. A marketing person at any reputable company would never send out a direct mail piece that had not been professionally written and designed, copyedited, proofread and reviewed internally, with many levels of approval depending on the size of the campaign. Yet many of these same marketers send out email messages to millions of customers without any of those same steps to ensure accuracy and quality. Just because the cost of sending an email is a fraction of the cost of sending a piece of direct mail doesn't mean you shouldn't take it seriously. In fact, the opposite is true. Because email is such a pervasive and powerful medium, we believe you should spend even more time and effort to make sure that every email initiative is done properly and professionally.

That's why, in this section, we'll cover the critical first three steps necessary to create effective email newsletters:

Chapter 1: Creating Email That People Want to Read
Chapter 2: Writing and Managing an Email Newsletter Program
Chapter 3: Designing and Formatting Emails for Maximum Performance

Chapter 1: Creating Email That People Want to Read

If our DailyCandy email isn't interesting, useful and entertaining, it won't get forwarded. Having the right mechanics helps, like send-to-a-friend, but all the bells and whistles are no substitute for quality content.

—Pete Sheinbaum, COO, DailyCandy, Inc.

People love to complain about advertising. But for all their complaining, they tolerate an amazing amount of it. People have made an unwritten deal with publishers and broadcasters that they will accept advertising in exchange for information and entertainment.

They agree to this deal whenever they buy a magazine, watch television, listen to the radio or go to a movie. For example, most TV viewers agree to accept eight minutes of commercials in exchange for twenty-two minutes of entertainment from half-hour sitcoms like *Everybody Loves Raymond*. Likewise, millions of people will happily pay $1.50 each day for the *New York Times* in spite of the fact that it is 70% advertising, because the other 30% is content that they find interesting, informative or entertaining. If the content is not entertaining or informative, they will change the channel or stop buying the newspaper. The same concept is true for email. If you don't provide compelling content, people will tune out, in this case deleting the email. Therefore, email has to rise to the challenge and be worth reading.

The sheer amount of clutter found in the average email inbox makes it that much more important to produce content that is not only worthwhile but that stands out. After fighting through a swelling wave of mortgage offers, online diplomas, and get-rich-quick schemes, consumers have little patience left over for emails that are uninteresting, even if they come from top brands or companies with which they do business.

The Three R's of Email Marketing: Relevance, Relevance, Relevance

People are selfish when it comes to what emails they choose to spend their time reading, because time is precious in our pressure-filled society. Therefore, it's not surprising that a study by ad agency Quris found that 80% of consumers stop reading emails they have signed up for because they deem them "irrelevant." And don't let a low unsubscribe rate fool you into thinking this doesn't happen to your program: in the same study, 93% of respondents reported deleting these irrelevant emails unread rather than unsubscribing. Worse yet, many of those people simply press the "this is spam" button provided by their ISP.

Make sure the content is relevant

Marketers always need to understand what the customer wants and needs in order to deliver on their promises. This is especially true for email newsletters. Customers are generally not interested in your third-quarter earnings (unless they are investors), where your new offices are located or how you make widgets. Readers want information that they can use, whether it's the latest fashion advice on how to dress for success or tips on writing their resumes. The content should therefore be about them, not you. Tell your readers how they can look better, where they can go on their next vacation, how to manage their time and finances, what they can do to beat their business competition, how they can make more money, raise their kids or even choose the best movie to see over the weekend. If your product or service can help them achieve these things, or anything else they desire for that matter, then you've got them.

However logical and proven this practice seems, most marketers use the opposite approach in planning their email content strategy, constantly going through the same self-serving and ineffective steps:

Step 1: What do we want to tell our customers?

Step 2: How can we get them to buy more of what we're selling?

Step 3: Which offer will make them want to buy our products (usually the same offer they can get in our retail store or online or through a sales rep)?

This is the wrong approach if you want to take advantage of the unique power of email as a way to build profitable long-term relationships with your customers. Instead, first figure out what your customers want to know. Ask them. Test alternatives. Watch your sales churn. Listen to customer comments and complaints. Then create a newsletter full of relevant content and weave your sales messages around that information. The results can be powerful.

The newsletter approach can work for ANY company, selling any product or service

Before we delve too much deeper, we want to disabuse you of the notion we encounter day after day: "Yeah, but newsletters won't work for us because…" We encounter this outlook particularly among business-to-business marketers, who sometimes see newsletters as a waste of time—both theirs and their audience's. But of course it's prevalent on the consumer side too, where "special offers" still rule the day. We'd like to share the example of a client we work with who has found a way to connect with its customers through newsletters.

Kimberly-Clark, as most people know, makes consumer-packaged goods, particularly paper products. They also have an industrial division, Kimberly-Clark Professional. Their customers are janitors, facilities managers and the like, who buy paper towels, toilet paper and so on for businesses, hotels and such. These products are generally sold through a distribution channel.

How on earth could they use email newsletters?

Easy. By figuring out what this audience cares about and then packaging it for them. Each month, Kimberly-Clark Professional produces an email newsletter called *The Link*. It features stories of interest to people working in facilities management. Recent headlines include "Energy Savings Reap Big Rewards," "Building Service Contractors Report High Levels of Job Satisfaction" and "Six Steps to Food Safety." Each issue includes a links to online tools, such as a Distributor Locator and a Towel Cost Calculator. And, of course, it has promotions for Kimberly-Clark products.

The newsletter is very popular with readers, enjoying an admirable average open rate of 30% and an average click-through rate of more than 41%—in fact, some editions have had a click-through rate as high as 65%! The content gets about twice the clicks that the promotions do, proving their worth in keeping the subscribers engaged and keeping the Kimberly-Clark brand in front of their customer base on a regular basis in a way that would be much more difficult if they only had the product ads. The trick, they've learned, is having the right mix of content and sales—content to keep people reading, promotions to drive sales.

Read on. Throughout this section you will find many more examples of all kinds of marketers using newsletters to market their companies' products and services to a dizzying array of audiences. And trust us, you can find a way to make it work for your business, too.

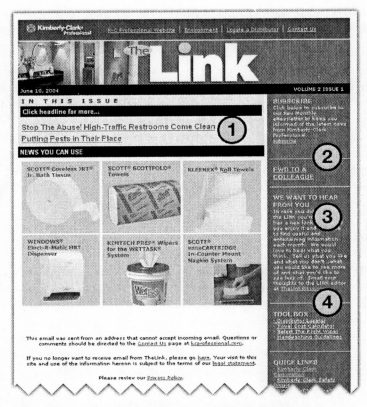

Kimberly-Clark's *The Link* proves that you can find the right content for any audience. In this case, they are trying to reach facilities managers. They do so by honing in on their very specific concerns. Each issue contains content that will be compelling to their readers (1) and (4). They also give prominent placement to subscribing to the newsletter, forwarding to a colleague (2) and calling for feedback (3).

Make sure the language is relevant

Always keep in mind that you need to "speak in the customers' language," especially when writing for a niche market. It's imperative to know the terminology and lingo, buzzwords (or lack thereof) and current and upcoming trends.

The tone of your email should reflect both the subject matter and the culture that surrounds the topic. It also needs to reflect the level of competence your target audience has regarding the subject matter. For example, a medical newsletter written for doctors and nurse practitioners might use more detailed medical terminology and discuss more complex issues than a health care newsletter designed and written for lay persons. Likewise, if you're selling casual clothing to teens or young adults, your wording will be much different than if you are selling designer suits to senior executives.

Studies have shown that phrasing is crucial to marketing success. If you state, "We've discovered a new anti-aging medicine," you'll receive a positive response from curious readers. If, however, you say, "You can stop the aging process with our new discoveries," you'll draw an even larger audience, because you are not only featuring the subject but also empowering the readers. That's quite an accomplishment for just one phrase. The message remains the same, but once you give the subject of the sentence to them as opposed to "we" "us" or "I," you are targeting the reader—and that's important.

One last point on relevance: always, always, always stay on top of feedback. If feedback or comments indicate that you are missing out on a trend in the industry, you probably are, so look into it. It's one of the best ways to remain relevant to your audience. We'll go into detail about profiting from feedback in Chapter 6.

Editorial Quality Matters

Quality means providing something that is worthwhile and exciting to your audience. That's why you shouldn't just hand the writing of your newsletter over to your marketing or PR department if they're not experts in creating compelling email newsletters. Hire an experienced writer who can put a spin on the content and offer a unique approach to the subject. It will make all the difference in the world. It may be trial and error at first, but in time your writer—with help from yourself and everyone else involved in the newsletter—will be able to determine what content your readers desire most. Provide what readers desire and your number of subscribers will go up. Readers will forward your newsletter to friends, who in turn will subscribe and forward it to more friends.

As part of your dedication to editorial quality, you should also make sure that your email newsletter builds a sense of familiarity with your readers by publishing on a regular schedule and making sure that your newsletter has a consistent and familiar look and feel. We'll go into more detail on these two points in Chapters 2 and 3, respectively.

Make It a "Magazine"

Compare the email that your company sends out to the Sunday newspaper. Is it more like the wad of coupons that gets taken out and tossed almost immediately, or is it like the magazine section that gets set aside and pored over? If your emails rival the magazine section, then you are providing content that people will read and discuss with their friends and colleagues.

Don't let the word "magazine" intimidate you. This is simply an editorial approach. You don't need lots of pages, nationally-recognized columnists and glossy photos. A few paragraphs of content is usually more than enough for an email. The content simply needs to be relevant and draw the readers' attention.

The "newsletter" concept serves this purpose well, which explains why there are numerous email newsletters. Research shows that they are actually more effective than mere advertising coupons or promotional flyers. When you want your newsletter to build your business, think of the content as a very important lead-in to your marketing and sales messages. To that end, remember that people expect to see a good deal of advertising when they buy a magazine. As long as the content is worthwhile, not only will they not mind the ads, they may even pay more attention to them as they read the magazine. The same holds true with your email. If your content is good, you can promote the needs, desires and benefits that drive the purchase of your product—in addition to surrounding it with ads and promotions—and readers won't mind at all.

Sell Tastefully, but Sell Everywhere

As we just discussed, if your content is good, readers won't mind your ads. Keep in mind, however, not to bombard your audience only with blatant advertise-ments—sell tastefully, but feel free to sell everywhere. Some of the best places to sell:

- **In your action areas:** "Action areas" are spaces in the newsletter that gen-erally have the highest click rates, such as the top left and right corners. Put your best offers here and rotate their placement to see which offer draws the best response from each spot.

- **Between stories:** As long as the distinction between an ad and your content is clear, it is perfectly acceptable to place ads within the content. Some publishers even break stories mid-sentence to insert an ad. That can, however, be distracting or annoying to readers, so use your judgment.

- **In the footer**: Once the reader has finished reading your newsletter, use the space at the bottom to feature more information about your company and products. It's a great opportunity to feature all of your company's information (since that's where most readers assume such information resides). The footer is also an ideal placement for secondary promotions, since it will not interfere with your main messages.
- **In the header**: While most of the space at the top of the newsletter should be reserved for branding (your company name and publication title), you can also use this space to place links to special offers on your web site.
- **In sidebars**: Often, sidebars offer the best mix of prominence and separation. But this option is available only in HTML templates, so make sure your text template can accommodate this advertising elsewhere.

A perfect example of a smart balance of content and advertising is Beech-Nut's monthly newsletter. It features content that is relevant to the age of the recipient's child. It includes fun games that parents can play with their children, expert advice on hot topics and helpful parenting tips. Running down the left-hand side are plenty of ads for Beech-Nut products. The focus is on the needs and wants of the reader, but in a way that supports the sales objectives of the company. This is the perfect marriage between content and commerce.

You can also advertise within your content by inserting plugs for yourself, or your products or services (the Beech-Nut newsletter does mix in references to specific products with some of the content), but always pay attention to the value proposition to the reader: if the content begins to read as a shameless plug or a long advertisement, you will lose your readers.

Make It Interactive with Surveys

Surveys give readers a sense of involvement and ownership. They draw people in and give them a piece of the action by allowing them a chance to be heard. They also allow you an opportunity to learn about your readers and create demographic data. In fact, a study conducted in May 2004 by ChoiceStream, a provider of personalization solutions, revealed that more than half of U.S. adults would share their demographic information and preferences to receive personalized web content and services. Overall, the survey results suggest that U.S. consumers are willing to offer up their personal data to companies that will use it to tailor their online offerings based on this knowledge, delivering more relevant content on each visit. We talked earlier about consumers' unwritten "deal" with publishers and broadcasters to accept advertising in exchange for information and entertainment. This modern exchange of personal information for custom content is the "New Deal" in the online media.

Each time you feature a survey, you have the opportunity to add more information about your readers, slowly build up your database and, most important, keep your content relevant.

Newsletters Aren't the Only Emails You Can Send

While the focus of this book is how to create and send valuable, content-filled newsletters, we're not suggesting that this is the only type of email you should ever send. While newsletters are the cornerstone of a great email marketing campaign, there are other types of email you will likely want or need to send, including event invitations, shipping and order confirmations and account information. And yes, a good program even has room for a few purely promotional blasts. In fact, once you have established a firm relationship with your client base, promotions such as coupons can be hugely successful. A case in point is Hormel, the manufacturer and marketer of highly popular consumer-branded food products. They worked with CoolSavings to offer promotional coupons via email and saw amazing results. Nearly 50% of consumers who took an action on Hormel's promotion printed three or more coupons. And 53% of consumers who reported redeeming a coupon also purchased at least one or more incremental Hormel products without a coupon.

While coupons might be the ultimate in direct response, CoolSavings has also proved their power in branding. For example, they did a program with 3M to use email coupons to build awareness and drive trials of two new products. The results were incredible: email recipients who printed coupons were between 263% and 271% more likely than those not exposed to the campaign to consider purchasing these products. And the branding lift extended to consumers who didn't print—they were between 14% and 20% more likely to consider a future purchase.

The problem is, a lot of companies only send ads, and that leads to ever-diminishing returns. People get tired of the continuous barrage of ads and either tune you out or unsubscribe. Furthermore, some people will simply never read ads. The key is to synergize. Balance your program so you're sending content-based emails that excite and create desire, promotions that make sales and confirmations that bring the money home.

© Copyright 2004 CoolSavings, Inc. All Rights Reserved.
Reprinted with permission.

Coupons can be cool—really. CoolSavings uses a crisp, clean layout to deliver Hormel's money-saving offers in a powerful fashion. The message is clear. The printing method is easy and obvious, and the results, as reported above, speak for themselves.

Lessons from the Inbox:
Email as Part of an Integrated Marketing Effort

All seasoned marketers understand the importance of a properly integrated marketing campaign. The benefits are obvious. Such a campaign cuts across media boundaries and reaches your audience wherever they may be. Email is a critical part of any integrated marketing effort because, as we mentioned earlier, email has become an important part of our society. People use email to conduct business, socialize and organize their personal lives. And thanks to portable handheld email devices, many people have access to email all day, virtually anywhere. This makes it imperative that every serious marketer have a focused email effort that continues to reinforce the brand, promote sales and reinforce relationships in this all-important medium. For marketers, ignoring email as a major marketing medium is like being in the shipping business and ignoring trucks. In fact, as you continue through this book, you'll be able to make the case that—depending on the type of business—email is the most prominent marketing vehicle in the mix.

Chapter 2: Writing and Managing an Email Newsletter Program

We have definitely seen the efficacy of mixing content and commerce in email. We have seen improved results by adding more offers to newsletters that had been primarily content, and by adding content to emails that had been primarily offers. The marriage of the two is what works.

—Gretchen Harding, marketing manager, BabyCenter

Every marketer should also be a good publisher. Why? Because publishers are experts at using content to create a platform and an environment for selling all sorts of products and services relevant to their readers. This means a lot more than *writing* great copy, although we will talk about ways to achieve that. It is about structuring your email program so that the content you send entices and creates anticipation—and, most importantly, that it *sells*.

There are many elements that go into producing such a program. For starters, there must be some really good, relevant content ideas that form the basis of your overall content strategy. Then someone must sit down, put pen to paper (or fingers to keyboard) and write content that subscribers don't simply want to read but want to act upon, which means making purchases or forwarding your email to friends. And this process must be carefully managed so that it can be repeated successfully for each newsletter, the end result being an effective campaign. But how? In this chapter, we'll cover how to do just this.

What to Write: The Secrets of Quality Content

As mentioned in the previous chapter, your content must, first and foremost, focus on the interests of your readers. Newsletters that are strictly about your products or services will eventually fail. While every email effort you make is ultimately about your brand, always remember to connect your content directly to the lifestyle and interests of the reader. Readers need to be able to relate to your message and easily see how it has a positive impact on their lives. If they can't buy it, wear it, hear it, eat it or use it to suit their needs or help them achieve their personal or professional goals, then they simply won't be interested.

The smartest way to accomplish your sales goals and still stay relevant is to write content that *implies* what you sell rather than blatantly promoting your products or services. For example, if your content talks about how to dress for success, it should mention that your line of clothing not only meets these criteria, but that it is also easily purchased online. If your content teaches how to grow a healthier garden using a certain type of fertilizer or ground treatment, your readers will learn something that is of benefit to them. Then help them easily find and purchase the related fertilizers or ground treatments your company sells by putting ads in the sidebar, header and footer of the newsletter.

Publishing a newsletter is all about hooking your readers. Educate them, entertain them, enlighten them and make it easy for them to act on their needs and impulses. Do this and they will welcome your emails. What's more, you will create top-of-mind positioning for your brand that the reader will rely on whenever the need arises for the type of product or service that your company provides. This is part of what makes a good email marketing program so powerful: the opportunity to drive both immediate sales and long-term brand recall at the same time.

General Newsletters vs. Specific Newsletters

A general newsletter is a great way to get started, especially if your audience is diverse. You can use a general-interest newsletter to promote a wide variety of offerings and see what works. Most often, marketers start off with a general newsletter to build an email list. Then, by tracking open rates, readership, clicks, responses and feedback, as well as by using surveys, marketers can learn more about the specific interests of the audience and create more specialized newsletters to address those interests.

If your audience is already well defined, it may be smarter to start with a niche newsletter, as these can be easier to market and differentiate from those of the competition. In addition, a tightly focused newsletter that is of interest only to a specific group is ideal for very specialized offers or for helping to drive more complex sales.

A niche newsletter also allows you to become the big fish in a smaller pond. For example, it's easier to be the best email newsletter about classic films from the 1940s and 50s than it is to be the best email newsletter about film in general. In this manner, you establish yourself as the leader in a small market and create a strong base from which to build or expand.

Depending on the nature and size of your business, and the diversity of your audience, you can determine which approach will work best for you.

Military.com shows how general and specific newsletters can be used to target different segments of the same customer base. *Army Insider* is a general-interest newsletter that conveys the "goings on" in the lives of soldiers. As such, it's a great way to market almost any product or service—for example, long-distance telephone service or newsmagazines—to those active in the army. On the other hand, the *Careers* newsletter is focused on military personnel who are preparing to leave or who have already left the military and are concerned with civilian careers and business opportunities. Because the content is highly relevant to this group, it is an ideal vehicle for targeted ads for employment services, career counselors, realtors and financial services.

How to Come Up with Content Ideas That Pique Interest

We've already established that your newsletter has got to be compelling, engaging and enticing. Don't panic. It's not a daunting task. All you need to do is tap into the wellspring of quality content ideas that exists inside your (and every) company.

Start a content log, or idea archive, where you can file possible topics for future editions of the newsletter. Rather than trying to force ideas when it comes time to write each issue, use the archive as a repository to store those great story ideas that come to you on the ride to work, during meetings and hallway discussions, while you are reading other publications or even during lunch. Write down every idea—good or bad, refined or raw—and file them away for later. This way, you'll have many ideas to browse through when it's time to write the next newsletter. What's more, if you choose to write each issue with a theme in mind, you can browse the archive, looking at individual ideas and thoughts, and themes will begin to emerge.

Another great way to generate ideas is to get the people in your company involved in the process of creating the newsletter. Try offering rewards or recognition to employees who come up with ideas that get turned into actionable content. Start an email box or an intranet suggestion form so that everyone knows how to send ideas in to your content log. Try particularly hard to involve the folks who speak to customers—sales, customer service, executives and receptionists. They will have great ideas based on actual customer comments and interactions. As word gets out, even employees not normally involved in the newsletter process will know where to go if they've got an idea to share. This leads to a wider selection of story ideas for your newsletter writers. It also serves as an excellent motivating tool, since everyone loves to see their ideas in print.

There are many resources for content. Consider some of these:

- Ask your company's own internal experts for their ideas.
- Scour trade publications for trend stories to which you can add a unique and relevant extension or example.
- Read the feedback or letters from your customers.
- Invite happy customers to be interviewed for case studies.
- Survey customers or industry leaders, and publish the results.
- Ask industry experts to write a short article, or interview them, for your newsletter.
- Include excerpts from books or magazines (with permission, of course).
- Feature articles from content or community web sites. (Again, you'll need permission or a licensing agreement.)
- Highlight interesting facts or tidbits from advertisers or strategic partners.

Remember that there are many organizations that will be willing to give you content—either for a fee or in exchange for the exposure they might get from your newsletter. Don't be afraid to ask! As long as you secure permission and give proper credit, nothing is off limits.

Coming Up with an Original Angle

Even the most exciting subjects become boring if presented in the same way time after time. Think of ways to present your information that differentiate you from your competitors and even from other news sources, including newspapers and online portals.

Finding new and innovative ideas isn't difficult. For example, we know of a newsletter publishing company that was trying to reach employment recruiters in one of the most desirable areas in the U.S., New York City. They knew that creating yet another job-postings email would fail, as there were already too many out there. To stand out, they decided to take the resumes they had received and rewrite them into the style of personal ads. They then created a newsletter that resembled an online dating service. The response was very favorable. The content was witty, yet it still provided the important information. Subscribers forwarded the newsletter to their colleagues, and pretty soon most of the recruiters in New York City had signed up for this innovative newsletter. Not surprisingly, the advertising revenue followed.

Making Your Email Viral by Creating Content That People Want to Pass Along

Just like the famous shampoo commercial, there are numerous instances where consumers want to tell a friend, who then tells a friend, who tells another friend, and so on. To create something that will start such a viral chain reaction requires—you guessed it—quality content. Relevant content is always more likely to get forwarded than advertisements. When you deliver really compelling content, not only will your audience enjoy reading it, more often than not they will share it with friends. Email makes this incredibly easy, with the conveniently-located "forward" button. As we'll cover in another chapter, getting your subscribers to forward your email to their friends is a terrific way to build your subscriber base and increase your brand reach. So, when coming up with content, keep in mind some of the things that folks tend to forward to their friends. Of course, the content needs to imply the benefits of your products and be flanked by discrete promotional messages to be most effective.

There are numerous examples of effective content that will get passed along from reader to reader. Moms love sharing interesting parenting tips, executives share the latest business news and online gamers share new-release information and cheat codes. Any target market you select will have some prime focus of interest that they "must share with others." Your job is to determine what the viral start button is for your target audience.

So, what will people pass along? What "must share" content can you develop? While there is no sure-fire answer, here are some ideas to help you get rolling:

- **Inside information**: People like to feel that they have inside information, tips or news, or that they have discovered something unique that their circle of friends, family or business associates have not yet seen.

- **Industry information**: People will always forward items that might be helpful to their professional colleagues. MarketingSherpa, for example, has determined that their audience of marketing executives loves to share case studies, results data and articles to stay on top of the latest industry news. By creating a newsletter with content that is valuable to their audience and encouraging recipients to share it with colleagues, MarketingSherpa has built a list of 173,000 marketing, advertising and public-relations professionals.

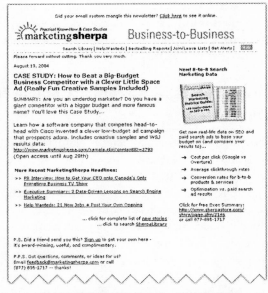

MarketingSherpa, a publisher of paid content for marketers, knows that their audience wants case studies, and they deliver! They use email as the principal distribution vehicle for their content—but they don't stop there. Knowing how busy marketing folks are, and the likelihood that they'll miss an issue, they provide links to related past content, available for a fee.

- **Ecards:** Ecards have been an extremely successful means of viral marketing. Blue Mountain Arts, featuring a variety of electronic cards that are sent to friends and family for birthdays and other occasions, has enjoyed phenomenal success. You can produce your own email cards without great expense. Lifeway Christian Resources, for example, ran an ecard promotion that gave each sender a map of the world. As their ecard was sent and then forwarded, virtual pins were added to the map to show where the ecard had been forwarded. The sender got the satisfaction of seeing how far they could spread the Gospel. Think of the occasions that make the most sense for your audience: new baby, wedding, get well and holidays are all popular themes, and cards for them can be easily created, with a place to include a personal message and some room for discrete marketing.

- **Inside jokes:** Jokes also work very well. But not just any jokes. Too many people are tired of the well-traveled routine jokes that land in their inbox from their aunt in Pittsburgh. You can, however, tailor your humor to fit your readers. Create tasteful, inoffensive jokes that appeal specifically to your audience. If you sell educational products, for example, an email with jokes specifically written to appeal to teachers is ideal. Not only will teachers appreciate it, but they will likely forward these jokes to other teachers, who will appreciate the inside humor. This will quickly result in an extensive list of quality leads.

- **Games:** Particularly when marketing to a younger crowd, games are a terrific and relatively inexpensive way to capture attention and build awareness. There are plenty of companies that develop downloadable games that you can post on your web site. In fact, according to an article in the *Wall Street Journal Online*, when DaimlerChrysler's AG Jeep division wanted to promote a new version of its Jeep Wrangler Rubicon, they created a fun online game in which players could steer a Jeep through all kinds of terrain. Within six months, 250,000 people had handed over their name and email address to Jeep just for the privilege of downloading the free game. Best of all, 40% of those indicated that they were interested in purchasing a Jeep!

- **Group ideas:** If your audience is likely to form a club around their favorite activity you can use it as an opportunity for one person to forward your emails to other club members. For example, a golf outfitter could offer to send discounts to the other three members of a golfer's favorite foursome. An investment newsletter could invite investment club members to sign up their club for investment tips.

- **Coupons and savings**: Coupons are a great means of viral marketing. Everyone likes sharing savings with someone they know. Krispy Kreme has enjoyed very tasty success with their viral campaign through their *Friends of Krispy Kreme* email newsletter. They offer coupons that can be redeemed for a free featured doughnut. They made the coupon offer easy to pass along to family and friends, which resulted in new members to their email list. The campaign was a huge success, increasing their mailing list by 71%!

- **Things that are worth their while**: People will gladly pass along your information if there's something in it for them. You can offer a simple incentive program for forwarding an email to ten people, such as a coupon, a fun download, reward points, or something else of value to your audience. One of your advertisers or partners might be happy to provide you with a discount to offer to your subscribers if it drives business their way. One caution: As with any incentive, you risk that your prize is more of a draw than membership to your newsletter. Some participants will only stay on your list long enough to reap the reward and then unsubscribe or ignore future mailings. Rewards will never generate the same committed audience as quality content.

- **Off-beat stories**: If you intentionally conclude an otherwise business-oriented newsletter with a silly story, you increase the likelihood of having the newsletter, or that specific story, forwarded. The fun story prompts the forwarding of the entire content set, and your marketing messages go along for the ride. You can even build an entire newsletter around such stories. A case in point is *Strange but True*, a newsletter for human-resources professionals from our client BLR. The newsletter features unusual and entertaining stories that deal with various workplace scenarios, such as a recent story which documented the odd but actual happenings between toll collectors and drivers. *Strange but True* actually began as a final story in another of BLR's newsletters, but it became so popular that it demanded its own venue.

- **Other popular favorites**: Surveys, contests, cartoons, trivia and polls are all frequently forwarded. A case in point is a web site called YouThink.com, which offers free blogs and journals. This site has built an ever-growing list of dedicated users, many of whom were first attracted by the fun and entertaining quizzes and trivia games circulated via email.

Testing several of the methods above will help you determine which will be most effective for your audience. Try to work such viral material into your marketing campaign. You'll be amazed at the results it can generate.

Win a Free Website!

Enter to win a free website valued at over $2,000 compliments of Web 1 Dental, a leading developer of dental websites and Internet marketing programs.

> *"An effective website is no longer a convenient option, but a necessity for doctors seeking to maximize their practice's growth potential."*
>
> *- Bob Levoy*
> *"201 Secrets of a High Performance Dental Practice"*

Enter to Win On-line: Simply copy this URL into your Internet browser and type in your contact information: www.web1dental.com/FL.

A comprehensive well designed website can give your practice a competitive advantage, create greater patient loyalty and increase referrals.

Best Wishes and Good luck!

Bob Farbotko
Senior Vice President, Sales
Booth #1404, Florida National Dental Convention

The website winner will be drawn on June 17, 2006 at the Florida National Dental Convention. Feel free to stop by our booth (#1404) or view our services online at www.web1dental.com. You do not need to attend the conference or be present at the drawing to win.

What Not to Write

Simple. Avoid content that has no meaning or value to the reader. This includes company news, press releases and promotional and marketing information that doesn't tie into the purpose of the newsletter. Ask this of everything you write for your newsletter: "Will my readers care about this?" If the answer is anything but a resounding "yes," give it the axe.

Over time, we see newsletters that once featured quality content begin to give way to more and more promotional and marketing material. This often happens despite the fact that the program is working, usually because some higher-up in the organization sends down an edict like "Double revenues through email by the end of the quarter," which is hard to do without resorting to almost spammer-like tactics. While this may cause a quick spike in sales, this kind of activity can also lead to readers hitting the unsubscribe button in droves, costing you over the long term.

Also, when the temptation to use just any company news hits you, just say no. Be sure it's newsworthy and has a content-related reason to be a part of your newsletter. Or, integrate the product announcement into a content story by discussing current trends or events that will engage readers. Always remember that readers sign up for a newsletter as part of an unwritten agreement: They expect interesting or valuable content from you (which just happens to be surrounded by advertising and marketing messages). As soon as you stop holding up your end of the bargain, you'll lose readers.

How Much to Write

People like nugget-sized information, and even depend on it, especially when so many view their email on handheld and mini-email readers. Therefore, make your newsletter concise and to the point, and make it very easy to skim by using headlines and subheads to help the reader along.

Research has found that newsletters with several short stories typically get read more often than emails with one long story, which is frequently saved for later and then often deleted unread. Always, always, always remember that, in today's world, time is in incredibly short supply, and people will see a long story as requiring too much of a commitment unless it is of immense interest or importance to them personally.

An email with several short stories gives people a choice as to what they want to read, whereas a one-story email is a hit-or-miss proposition. If the reader doesn't like the one story you provide, you've lost him.

Don't doubt your ability to convey a message in a short two- or three-paragraph story. Boil it down to the key message, use bullet points, and offer a link to more detailed information on your web site. This is also a great way to drive traffic back to your site. Just make sure that the email content can stand on its own, so you aren't annoying your readers.

If you can't shorten the story, a good strategy is to serialize your content. In other words, break a long story into several short stories. Decades ago, the publishing world used to serialize novels by printing two or three chapters and selling them weekly or monthly. This would build anticipation among readers and have them yearning for the next installment. You can apply the same idea to your newsletters and leverage the same excitement.

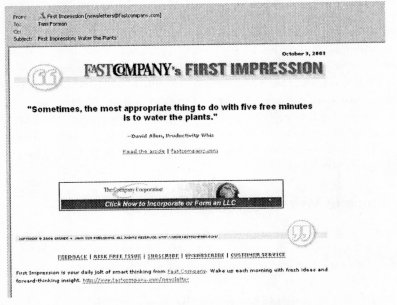

By Keith Hammonds, © 2004 Gruner + Jahr USA Publishing. First published in
Fast Company Magazine. Reprinted with permission.

You don't need a lot of content to create a compelling email newsletter. Fast Company's *First Impression* newsletter consists of just one interesting quote from a feature article. Because the quote is always fun, quirky or provocative, they keep readers interested without overwhelming them.

Who Should Write Your Newsletter?

Perhaps we should start with who should *not* write your email newsletter. As we mentioned previously, avoid making the obvious choice of using someone in your PR or marketing department, since most people who are great at writing sales and promotional copy are not typically adept at writing interesting content that will hook readers. Often, these professionals will find themselves drifting into the inevitable habit of selling or promoting products and services, or writing from the company's perspective. Instead, use these internal resources to help you understand your target audience and develop your story ideas, then turn over the duty of crafting the actual newsletter copy to a writer.

It should go without saying that it makes no sense whatsoever to have the tech guys who send the email write the email—even if you are writing to a tech audience. Would you have your printer write your direct-mail piece? Anyone involved with technology or design should not be involved with writing.

The best option: A freelance writer

Unless you have professional writers on staff for other reasons, your best option is a freelance writer. This is a professional or journalist who is skilled at turning out creative, high-quality content. Freelance writers cannot only provide the talent you need, but they are also quite affordable, because they aren't employees and work on an as-needed basis. This is often the best option for creating great email newsletters without straining internal resources or increasing headcount.

Find a freelance writer who is somewhat familiar with your area of business or the topics you want to write about. Although he or she shouldn't be expected to know all of the details, a good writer should be able to do in-depth research (including tapping your public relations, marketing, tech guys and other executives in your company) and find material for the newsletter. While freelancers are not as great a risk or investment as full-time hires, you still want to screen them thoroughly. Read some of their published writing samples and check references.

It is best to use only one writer for either your whole program or at least for each individual newsletter so that the tone and style of your newsletter will be consistent and will work to enhance your brand. What's more, a regular writer will also become familiar with your audience, which will lead to more effective writing.

To find a good freelance writer, ask for references from your PR and marketing department, or go online and check some of the many posting boards that advertise the services of professional freelance writers.

Why You Should Publish More Than One Newsletter

As we mentioned in the section on general vs. specific newsletters, it makes sense to start with one newsletter to get the program going. But over time, as you learn more about your readers, you'll want to add more to deliver content to target-specific segments of your audience. There are four chief reasons to send multiple newsletters:

"Unsubscribe insurance"

With one newsletter, a given email address is either on your list or not on your list. By offering multiple newsletters, you have the ability to generate multiple lists, and enable consumers to choose among them, thus preventing the all-or-nothing scenario.

Self-segmentation

No matter how sophisticated your back-end databases are, they are no substitute for the declared preference of a consumer. Let them tell you what they want instead of guessing or applying formulas. For instance, let's assume you're a large, multi-channeled retailer and you have a subscriber who is a young urban professional female. Demographic segmentation would dictate that you send her email that addresses fashion, home furnishings and high-tech gadgets. If she once bought tools as a gift for her father, behavioral segmentation would demand that you begin to send this person content about tools, tents and kitchen appliances.

But if you allow this buyer to select her own email offerings, she may very well choose to receive emails pertaining to the areas of outdoor sports and toys—a topic that didn't fit either profile—for her nephews, who you never knew existed. Not only does this tactic offer another avenue of contact with this customer, but because she selected the topic herself she is more likely to open and act upon these emails. Moreover, because she selected the topics, she'll be anticipating your emails. What a great start to a mutually beneficial relationship!

Better opportunities for contextual targeting

When it comes to email, specific always outperforms vague. With one-size-fits-all permission, you are forced to write weak copy and provide "special offers" for general merchandise. By creating a set of distinct mailings, you will be able to write crisp, specific marketing copy around each that will speak to the user, boosting readership and increasing your response and revenue.

Increase volume without increasing spam rage

You could never get away with blasting everyone on your list with email ads on a daily basis. But there are many people who will voluntarily sign up for five or more weekly newsletters, provided each is new, fresh and different. You can also vary frequency, format and more to get the right message to the right person every time. A client once told us that sending twice as many email ads would "obviously" generate twice the revenue. This is very limited thinking. At first, revenue will increase. But over time, the risk increases that you will turn off your recipients. A better way is to offer the option of additional newsletters, thus giving customers a reason to actually want more email from you.

The key to coming up with ideas for additional newsletters lies with your customers. Monitor their behavior. If people who visit your travel site are constantly clicking on stories about cruises, then start a specific newsletter featuring content about taking a cruise. Offer suggestions on how to dress while onboard a cruise ship, activities to try onboard, reviews of cruise food and other related topics. Analyze the areas of your site that generate the most interest and then create targeted, well-written newsletters to match. Or simply ask them. Include a survey in your next email newsletter (or on your sign-up form), and ask your customers what else they'd like you to offer.

How to Use the "Unsubscribe Flip"

As we just mentioned, one of the best reasons to have multiple newsletters is that you don't necessarily lose a subscriber completely when they tire of one newsletter. Instead, by using what we call the "Unsubscribe Flip," as they go off of one list, you can entice them to go right onto another. The key to making this technique work is to offer the subscription check-boxes for all your lists right on your unsubscribe page. You will usually get a new subscriber for every one who unsubscribes. For example, if you look at women's portal iVillage's unsubscribe page, you'll find they offer dozens of newsletters. When a reader is leaving one list, odds are she'll see something else she wants.

Remember that an unsubscribe request is not a rejection of your company or content. That subscriber may just be busy or tired of the topic. By offering a variety of email choices, you stand a much better chance of keeping the lines of communication open.

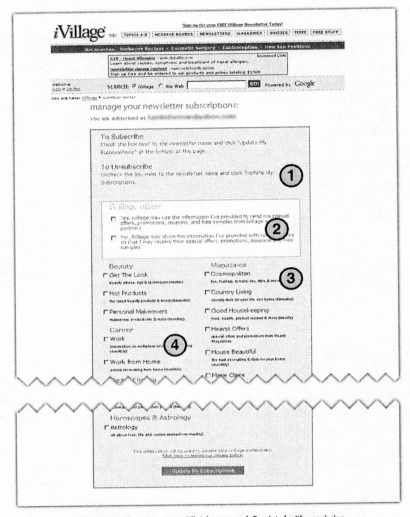

iVillage has a great email preference center, which serves two purposes: It helps interested subscribers find and subscribe to other newsletters of interest, and it is also the unsubscribe page. So, if someone wants to unsubscribe to a certain newsletter, the process is clear (1), but so too are the compelling reasons to stay on the list (2). In addition, great content, such as big-name magazines (3) and topical information (4), is available for fast browsing. Certainly, someone will be able to find at least one other topic of interest on this list.

How Often to Send Your Newsletters

Typically we recommend short newsletters, sent weekly. A weekly newsletter will keep your brand in front of the reader on a regular basis. It will become something they can bond with and expect to see on a specific day of the week. It will also allow you to remain current while not irritating your subscribers. Plus, it's usually not overwhelming to produce fifty-two short newsletters a year. If you follow the advice above and send more than one weekly newsletter, try to stagger them so they do not all arrive on the same day.

Some newsletters can remain popular on a biweekly basis. However, mailing less frequently than biweekly will diminish the branding value of the campaign, as people won't bond with it or learn to anticipate it.

Daily newsletters are only valuable if you have the content to support them and there is immediacy around the topic. If you are providing horoscopes, weather, or breaking daily news (including industry news), you can justify a daily newsletter. Sometimes even a quick blast, such as a daily tip, quote, idea or joke, can be a great way for people to start their day. Dilbert sends a daily comic, many financial services companies send stock tips daily and Comedy Central sends a very popular joke of the day.

Let your readers decide

Rather than agonize over how often to send your newsletter, let your readers decide. Simply offer them several options on your sign-up form, asking how often readers want to get your email (daily, weekly or bi-weekly). This way, people can select their own preferred mail volume. As well, put these same choices on your unsubscribe page. You'll be surprised how many readers choose to get mail less often instead of unsubscribing altogether. You can even offer users the option of putting their subscription on hiatus for a month or two. That way, people who are going on a long vacation or who just want a break for a while have the option of pressing the "pause" button on their subscription.

Balance your newsletters and your promotions

If you also send promotion-only emails, plan to deliver them on different days and at different times than your content newsletters. This way you can avoid over-sending to the same readers on the same days. Keep in mind that they are already seeing your offers in the newsletters. Also remember that ads and the newsletter should each have a distinctive look so that customers can easily differentiate between them and, ideally, subscribe and unsubscribe separately from them.

The master mailing calendar

One of the fastest ways to turn off readers is to inundate them with too much email, too often. Make sure that everyone in your company understands this. We had a client recently that couldn't understand why he received so many complaints about the volume of email that he sent out. After all, he only sent his email newsletter out weekly. After a bit of digging throughout the company, however, he discovered that the weekly newsletter from the marketing group was not the only email the company was sending these recipients. Three different groups within the company, in fact, were all sending emails to this group, unbeknownst to him. So while the recipients had only agreed to a weekly newsletter, they were receiving an average of fifteen emails a month, all from the same company. No wonder there were so many complaints!

You can stop this from happening at your company by creating a master email calendar so you can see clearly how often you are mailing to each list and when. Plus, by letting each department know your mailing schedule, you can do the following:

- Eliminate multiple mailings on the same day
- Allow other departments that might have material for the newsletter know when they need to have it prepared
- Protect your subscribers from being overwhelmed
- Improve and protect your customer service image

Getting Your Readers to Take Action

Of course, the desired end result of all of this effort is for your readers to act on the information you send to them. There are two critical actions that your readers must take. First, they need to open your email. This is your "open rate," and it is affected by both your subject line and your deliverability rate. Second, they need to respond to whatever offer or offers are included. This is known as the "click rate." There are a variety of strategies you can employ to accomplish each, which we cover below. We cover much more about how to measure your success when we discuss metrics in Chapter 7.

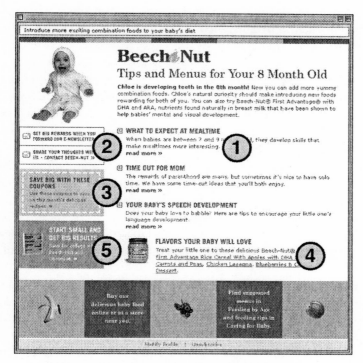

Beechnut's tips newsletter is loaded with terrific calls to action. As part of the promise, the important content is always first (1). Incentives are then offered for content ideas or for forwarding the newsletter to friends (2). There are printable coupons (3) and relevant new product information (4). There are even programs designed to help new parents save for college (5). This is a newsletter designed to generate results!

How to increase open rates

- **Focus on recognition**: Unknown emails are deleted almost instantly. If yours isn't recognized in an instant, it will never get opened, so stick to a common and consistent look, feel and publishing pattern, enabling readers to build an expectation for your messages.

- **Focus on the preview window**: Nothing matters more to recognition than what shows up in the preview window of your messages. Test different formats and offers to ensure that the most enticing and interesting information in your email appears at first glance. And be sure to keep in mind that the preview window will vary, so test your messages with a variety of different email programs, such as Outlook, AOL and Hotmail, and on a variety of screen sizes.

- **Keep a regular publishing schedule:** As we mentioned earlier, a regular publishing schedule makes it possible for readers to expect your email. Your readers come to anticipate them and reading them becomes a habit. If you toss your emails out randomly, you decrease the likelihood that recipients will treat them like a publication and develop a bond with them.

- **Never change the "From" address:** First, your "From" address is useful for user recognition. Second, it dramatically improves your chances of actually getting your email through the ISP spam filters and into the inbox. Plus, newer mail readers require or allow users to set a personal "whitelist"—a list of approved senders—based on the "From" address. If you change your "From" address, you run a much higher risk of getting blocked. There's much more on "From" addresses later in this Chapter.

- **Pay attention to your subject lines:** You want to focus your subject lines, like the content itself, on the interests and desires of your readers. It is generally effective to focus on the content of your email rather than the products or discounts. Don't be shortsighted: It's more important that they open the email than it is that you get in one more plug for your discounts. More specific advice on crafting great subject lines can be found in Chapter 3.

- **Don't include attachments:** People are more aware than ever of the havoc a virus can cause to their PC, and they know that most viruses are sent as attachments. That said, most emails with attachments—unless sent by a trusted friend or colleague—are automatically deleted. A better idea is to provide a link to a web page where a person can go to download a document. The end result is the same, and your email will have a better chance of getting delivered, read and acted on.

How to increase click rates

- **Make sure all actions are prominent:** Don't bury links or risk losing sales due to fancy designs that hide actionable links. No one clicks on what they don't see. Remember that all links and buttons should be very visible and stand out from the copy. Use action verbs such as "click," "buy" and "learn," and put actual images of buttons with these verbs on them to encourage more clicks. Always check every link in a newsletter before every mailing. And make sure all links are live, and that they're viewable in both text and HTML formats.

- **Offer alternatives to clicking**: Not everyone is online when they read your mail, so offer them the opportunity to respond in other ways. Always offer a phone number and, if appropriate, directions to a physical store. And make sure that your email address is prominent, so if a reader is offline (for example, on an airplane), she can craft an email message, on a laptop or portable email device, that will be sent when she gets back online.

- **Choose offers wisely**: Because relevance is the primary driver of email offer response, select offers based on customer lifecycle and behavior preferences. To ensure your offers are the most relevant, break your master list into multiple lists, segmented by demographics, geography and lifecycle.

- **Offer freebies**: Tell your readers about something they can't resist, and require that they come to your site to retrieve it. Maybe it's a coupon, a music download, a cool game or a hot new screen saver. Whatever it is, let them know why they have to have it and why they need to click through to get it.

- **Tout the stuff on your site**: A particularly popular method used by publishers is to add sections that directly promote valuable web site content. You can also add a box with "latest headlines" from the site. Write stories—or partial stories—that link directly to featured areas of the web site, and then link the story right to the hot spot on your site. Basically, use the email to do mini-reviews of your own content.

Lessons from the Inbox:
Email Preference Centers

When you get to the point where you are offering multiple newsletters to your subscribers, consider creating an email preference center, or a "Manage Your Subscriptions" page. Not only will this type of page help your subscribers clarify which newsletters they have agreed to receive, but if you list your other offerings, it may even spark the interest to sign up for more. What's more, it's a terrific way to forge a stronger relationship with your customers.

Your email preference center should include the following:

- Every email newsletter you offer, with an easy way to subscribe and unsubscribe (like a check-off box)
- A way to update subscriber profile or information
- An email change-of-address (ECOA) form
- A listing of the frequency of every mailing
- A tell-a-friend form
- A feedback link
- Prominent links to your privacy policy

You can include prompts for additional demographic information, such as gender, age, geographic location, household income, etc., but don't make this information mandatory or you risk losing any existing subscribers who wish to keep this information private. Promotions for product and services are also fine, but don't make them too prominent. Remember that your subscribers will view this as a management tool, not a marketing vehicle.

Making It Work

Even though your subscribers will view the email preference center as an administrative page, you always need to keep in mind that it is a key part of your overall email marketing initiative and should not be treated as an afterthought. It needs to encourage subscribers to stay on your lists while honoring all unsubscribe requests, all the while making the whole process fast and easy.

Think of it as the customer service desk at your favorite store: it's there to help you return things you don't like or need and find the things you do. Most importantly, it's always positioned in a place where you'll need to walk by some other great stuff first.

That said, don't forget to make it easy to find—promote it in your welcome message and email footers. Be sure that there are compelling calls to action for each newsletter. And of course, make it interactive with surveys or feedback forms.

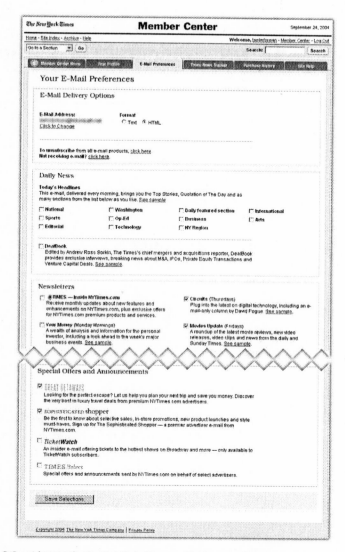

The *New York Times on the Web* offers an excellent example of an Email Preference Center. Everything is clear and simple—from email format preference to opt-ins for third-party offers—all on one page. Managing one's online account couldn't be easier! (See it for yourself at www.nytimes.com/email.)

Chapter 3: Designing and Formatting Emails for Maximum Performance

For us, the web site is the destination and our email newsletter is the gateway to the site. So we believe it's important for the newsletter to have a strong identity. If the reader doesn't recognize the newsletter within seconds, that door will close very quickly. Since we redesigned our templates we have yielded much higher open rates and at least doubled the click-through rates to our web site and editorial content. Now, we are looking at ways to change content offerings to push these rates higher. Once you have a template that works, tweaking other elements for better results becomes easy.

—Kristin Miller, ebusiness manager,
Kimberly-Clark Professional

Email: A Medium That Requires Special Design Considerations

Your approach to email design must be fundamentally different from print, direct marketing or even web page design. The reason is simple: your customers' experience with email is fundamentally different than with those other media.

Email design is not about the overall graphical impact but about scrolling, making it easy for the reader to skim and best utilizing a small space. This is why email demands a completely different approach and involves more effort than simply cutting and pasting material from a web site or converting your direct-mail campaign into HTML.

Email presents greater challenges for two reasons: first, because there is a need to design for the preview window as well as the entire message; and second, because people interact with email in fundamentally different ways and in different contexts than they do with other media. In fact, because readers scroll through email, it is important to think of the design as a series of modules. In addition, you have less control over the final rendering, because the software and hardware on the user's desktop (the various software programs or web browsers your customers use to view your message) will influence the final look and user experience.

Just as with any type of communication, if the design does not grab the attention of the reader or fails to present your message in an appealing way, you'll lose your audience. Therefore, email design plays a significant role in determining if the email will be read. In addition, readers will make split-second judgments as to whether or not to delete each email, so you must make sure that subscribers instantly recognize that the email is coming from you. An email newsletter that is well designed will ensure this.

Once that's accomplished, the design of your email must not only be appealing and make the recipient want to read it, but it must also allow the reader to skim the content and glean the key information.

Sound daunting? It can be. But it's easier when you break the process down into several key steps. In much the same way that your content strategy is about more than great writing, your email layout is about more than great design (although that is, of course, important too). It's about having the right elements in the right places to maximize the performance of every email you send.

The Importance of the "From" Address

The "From" address is the first thing subscribers will see in their email boxes. It needs to be immediately apparent that it is coming from a company they know and trust, and, more importantly, one from which they have agreed to receive emails. If they signed up for a newsletter from XYZ Widgets, they must quickly see "XYZ Widgets." Always use the company name that appears on the subscription form. This is especially important if the email is from the division of a company that has its own distinct brand name. For example, if someone signs up for a newsletter from Dell Publishing, which is a division of Random House, and they see Random House in the "From" address, they may not recognize it and will therefore be more likely to delete it. In that fraction of a second, they will not make the connection that this is the same company.

You also don't want the "From" address to be the name of someone working in the company, such as the newsletter editor or someone in customer service. This technique became popular based on the theory that people like to get email from other people rather than from companies. But with spammers using this technique more and more every day, folks have become wary of these techniques. One way to add a personal touch to your company moniker is to use titles, for example, "Dell Publishing Editors" or "Starbucks Baristas." And it doesn't even need to be an actual person or group of people; the point is to build recognition and enhance branding.

It's also important to note that many email blocking and filtering technologies use the "From" address as a way to identify spam, so changing the "From" address may very well increase the chance of having your email blocked or filtered. This is another reason, and perhaps the most important, that consistency and professionalism are important.

Consider This: Keys to Successful "From" Addresses
- Always use the exact company or division name with which the subscriber has signed up.
- Use a title to add professionalism and a personal touch.
- Avoid specific names of people, which most folks will ignore if unfamiliar.
- Consistently use the same information to breed familiarity, e.g., Dell Publishing Editors or Starbucks Baristas.

Subject Lines That Get Your Email Opened

Crafting the perfect subject line is a topic of much discussion and debate around the marketing water cooler because subject lines, along with the "From" address, have a tremendous impact on the open rate of your emails. If the subscriber doesn't use a preview pane, it is the only piece of information she has to determine if the email is worth opening. Here are some basic rules of thumb for crafting great subject lines:

- **Keep it as short as possible.** Many email readers (especially web-based readers) cut off long subject lines. The number of characters allowed varies. We recommend no more than fifty-five characters. Pay particular attention to the first fifteen characters, since they are the most visible in an inbox, especially those viewed on handheld devices.
- **Test often.** Creating winning subject lines is one of the easiest ways to improve campaign results. Test multiple approaches as often as you can. One of the great benefits of email is that you can test several subject lines on a small sample of recipients, and then send out your entire campaign an hour later using the subject line that gained the best results. We'll go into much more detail about testing in Chapter 6.
- **Skip spam words.** Spammers have stolen a lot of great direct-response words and phrases, such as "Free," "Discount," "Save," "Buy Now," and "Special Offer." As a result, these words will usually get your email blocked by spam filters. Be sure to test subject lines by sending your email

to test recipients with spam-checker software to make sure that your words are not causing your emails to be blocked from your subscribers' email inboxes. This issue matters both at the server level, where you'll get blocked by filters and corporate servers, and at the inbox level, where users will delete anything that looks even a little bit like spam. We will talk in more detail about filtering and other deliverability issues in Chapter 8.

- **Never use all capital letters.** In addition to being a classic spam technique that most filters will catch, it looks unprofessional, and users will more often than not delete them immediately. On a related note, don't deceptively use "RE:" or "FW:" in your subject lines to make it seem as if you are replying to the user—another classic, and unprofessional, spammer technique.
- **Be relevant.** Make sure not only that the line is enticing but that it also accurately reflects the relevant content your email contains. After all, that's why the subscriber wants your email. If that's not enough of a reason, consider that CAN-SPAM requires that your subject line at least not be deceptive.
- **Show value.** The subject line should state the value proposition, or what the reader will get from reading the message.
- **Add "zing" to your subject lines:** Be unique and enticing. Always remember that there are thousands of email marketing managers fighting for attention in that inbox. Don't settle for generic, bland subject lines. You are competing with every other email in the inbox, and you want to win. Put thought and attention into every subject line, and don't let it be the piece that gets written two minutes before the email goes out the door. Most importantly, resist the pressure to go for the safe choice or standard marketing line. "Don't Be Chicken—Try 10 New Recipes for Your Favorite Fowl" is way more fun than "Try 10 New Chicken Recipes." Zig when others zag and your message will stand out from the pack.
- **Put a number in the subject line:** What works for magazine covers also works for email. Readers respond to numbers. In particular, "top" lists are highly effective. We like "Top 10," but other numbers also work well in this format.

The subject line debate

Marketers have conflicting views as to whether it's more effective to use the same subject every time to increase recognition or to use unique calls to action to drive response. The honest answer is that it's different for every marketer, based on the type of content, the immediacy of the information and other factors, such as the mindset of your subscriber base. There are times when a consistent subject line works best. If you are selling the same service on a regular basis, there may be no need to switch subject lines. Other times, a changing subject line is recommended. For example, if you have special offers or hot breaking information, you will want to convey that sense of urgency to the reader.

We generally recommend combining the two approaches. By using a consistent lead-in (two or three words) followed by a colon and then a few words of copy that change for each message, you can provide a sense of consistency while still highlighting new goodies that will be featured in your latest issue. This works if you can avoid going over the character limits of most readers' email window. For example: "Garden News: Tulip Time! Get Planting Now." and "Garden News: Protect Your Plants from Frost." Both of these examples stick to a consistent theme while demonstrating variety, and they are under forty-five characters, including spaces. Military.com uses this technique to great effect, with their *The Early Brief* newsletter. Every issue begins with the name of the publication, then has four to six words to highlight the top story. Recent examples include "THE EARLY BRIEF—Baseballs Used for Troop Tribute" and "THE EARLY BRIEF— Military Housing Improving."

Using Headers to Build Interest and Recognition

The header is the design or copy at the very top of your email newsletter. It is what the recipient will see upon first glance at your newsletter, so its design is crucial. As we mentioned earlier, be sure that every newsletter features a similar look and feel so that readers can instantly recognize your email and be inclined to open and read it. In addition, it should also carry all vital identifiers, such as your company name and/or logo and the date, if it's relevant to the content. And make sure the headline for your top story isn't too far down, so your readers see it right away. Think of the top six inches of a broadsheet newspaper.

By creating interesting, consistent header designs, it is easy to quickly and easily identify a publication, its date, its issue and its top stories. Leverage that market conditioning for your own program, and think of the header as the "star of the preview window." This means that it acts the same way a web site masthead works, providing an image and major navigation. It also serves as a teaser, enticing and encouraging the reader to open the email and explore all of the wonderful information contained within.

One point to keep in mind when designing your newsletter is to avoid using dark backgrounds. While they may look nice, headers with dark backgrounds create typing problems when forwarded. (We'll cover the importance of having your emails forwarded in Chapter 4.)

Don't Forget about Footers

The footer, the text that appears beneath the actual newsletter content, is the best place for administrative messaging and CAN-SPAM compliance, but it also offers a great opportunity to continue to sell your products and services and to reinforce your branding. Too many marketers waste this opportunity. While this text is not a guaranteed read every time, many readers do scroll down for more information. Also, people who get an email forwarded to them will instinctively look to the bottom of the email to find out who sent it originally.

This is why standard information about your business, typically called a boilerplate, should always be included. And since this is a book about direct marketing, we'd be remiss if we didn't encourage you to use this space to drive some of your long-term marketing objectives by highlighting products on the horizon, or secondary offers. Be sure to include all of your key company information, including contacts, links to press releases and to your web site and of course promotions of your other newsletters.

It should go without saying—but we'll say it anyway—that your footer must include all the legal bits required by CAN-SPAM, including unsubscribe instructions and a postal address. And while CAN-SPAM requires a postal address, we say be brave and include a phone number, too. You'll be surprised that it will increase credibility rather than complaints. For more details on CAN-SPAM compliance, see Chapter 9.

Unlike the header and content, the footer copy does not carry the same mandate of brevity. Readers do not perceive this as part of the newsletter, so you can spread it out a little more.

Some of the elements we recommend including in the footer:

- An "About this newsletter" section
- An "About the company" section, with links back to the site
- Viral elements, including subscription forms and tell-a-friend forms
- Administrative elements, such as copyright and contact info
- A privacy policy mention or link
- Promotions for your other email newsletters
- Links to special features on your web site
- Subscribe, unsubscribe and account-modification links
- A teaser about content in your next newsletter
- A customer feedback link, of course

Consider This: Taking Offline Ideas Online

When you read a magazine or newspaper, you typically don't read the masthead. You do, however, know where to find it in case you need the information that it contains, such as the name of an editor or a phone number. The same is true with the footer of your email. Use it to your full advantage.

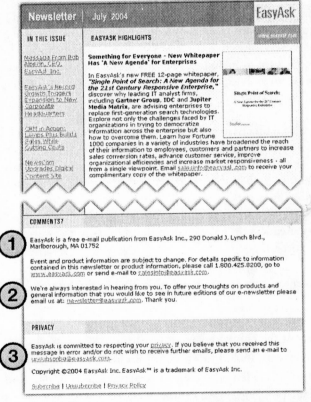

© Copyright 2004 EasyAsk, Inc. All rights reserved. Reprinted with permission.

EasyAsk makes excellent use of the footer in their *EasyAsk Highlights* newsletter. It includes a comfortable mix of administrative and marketing elements. Note how they make it easy to contact EasyAsk (1), provide feedback (2) and learn about their privacy policy and unsubscribe information (3). There is lots of valuable information in a clear yet unobtrusive place, so it doesn't conflict with the main content.

The Preview Window: Keeping the Good Stuff "Above the Fold"

"Above the fold" in email refers to what generally appears in a standard preview pane, such as in Microsoft Outlook or AOL. For readers who use this feature, the elements appearing here will primarily determine whether or not the email gets opened. If you grab the attention of the reader by what is in this small portion of the screen, you can hold their interest.

The preview pane is akin to the envelope of a direct mail piece, or the lead element in a direct-mail package. Taking full advantage of this space involves much more than displaying your corporate logo. You need to make sure that what the reader sees first is compelling, relevant and informative and that it offers a reason to open the message or scroll down. You only have a few seconds (at most!) before someone decides to delete an email, and that decision may be based on the first glance at the preview window.

We recommend that the following elements—usually the main parts of a good header—be kept "above the fold":

- Name of the publication
- Name of the company and logo
- Tagline, if you use one
- Volume and/or issue number
- Date
- Table of contents
- Significant headlines
- A link to your web site

If your table of contents is short, as it should be, you may include a few lines of content from one of your stories. While this serves as a teaser, you need to make sure the story continues immediately or with one click. Don't put items or teasers above the fold that won't be easily found once readers open and start reading the email.

You can also drive your readers to action by including graphics they can click on for more information, special offers and other goodies.

Always be aware that your subscribers are viewing your email on a myriad of email software programs. Even the most common, such as Microsoft Outlook, often have hundreds of variations, ranging from those for different versions of operating systems to those customized for corporations. Therefore, it's important to view your email in as many different formats as possible, particularly those that are small, such as on laptops and handhelds, since it is very important to determine exactly what your reader will see.

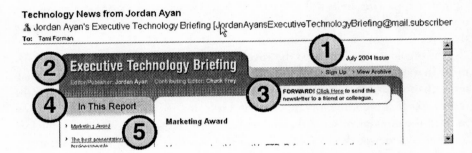

SubscriberMail's *Executive Technology Briefing* makes terrific use of the preview window. In just this small area, they've managed to provide the issue date (1), the newsletter title (2), a prompt to forward the message to others (3), a table of contents (4) and the top story headline (5). And because the newsletter is well designed, all of this information is presented in a clear, uncluttered format.

What to avoid in the preview window

- **A long, text-heavy story.** Readers will not jump right in and start reading. They are looking to skim. If you try to pack too much information above the fold, your email will appear cluttered.

- **Prominent third-party advertising.** If they see this information come up prominently above the fold, your subscribers are likely to think this is an email from another company, in spite of the "From" address.

- **Too much advertising for your own products and services.** If advertising dominates the layout, you run the risk of losing your audience. Remember, they've agreed to receive advertising as long as they also receive content of some value. If the newsletter has a good mix of both, as it should, then this value will be reflected in the preview area.

The Pros and Cons of HTML Emails

If you use HTML programming for your emails, you gain the ability to create a much richer graphic design than available in text-only emails. Many audiences react favorably to the graphic elements and design flexibility that HTML permits. HTML templates allow you to include the following:

- **Graphics and rich text:** HTML email gives you immense flexibility in your newsletter designs and provides you with the ability to create a rich look and feel.

- **Advertising:** You have the ability to place graphic ads throughout your newsletter—in the header, along the sidebars, in the footer and between your stories. By utilizing these spaces through the use of HTML, you can strategically place your ads in the positions where they'll be most effective.

- **Forms:** HTML allows you to put live forms into your newsletter so your readers can take action (e.g., subscribe, tell-a-friend) without having to leave your newsletter and visit the web site. Forms can, however, present some technical issues, so be sure to test any email forms before sending.

- **Tracking:** Because you can track subscriptions, referrals, click-throughs, and conversions through the use of an HTML template, you are able to do more sophisticated analysis of your campaigns. We'll cover much more about tracking and testing in Chapter 6.

Keep in mind though that while HTML offers many opportunities, it is also subject to pitfalls. Here's what to watch out for when designing an HTML newsletter template:

- **Design for design's sake:** Too often, graphic designers (and the rest of us!) try too hard to design something complicated and technically impressive and lose sight of the fact that the purpose of their newsletter is to communicate efficiently and effectively, sell products and drive their brand. Make sure your designer has a clear understanding of the purpose of the email and communicates regularly with the team that is driving the email newsletter initiative. The day of dazzling an audience with bells and whistles alone has passed. Subscribers demand substance, and design elements need to enhance the readability of that substance. Email design is not print design, or even web design.

- **Losing the space above the fold**: Make sure your layout is sized in such a way that no single item takes up all the prime space above the fold. It's more important to get all essential elements above the fold than to have big graphics, so get your logo and table of contents front and center so readers know why they should bother to look at the rest of the message.
- **Requiring downloads**: Never design your template so that a reader will be required to download any additional programs (e.g., Macromedia Flash) in order to view it. It's an unnecessary barrier for lots of users.
- **Getting blocked by some ISPs**: While this will not always be the case, there are some ISPs and corporate spam filters that will block emails that are too graphic intensive. Most email messages come in at about 10 to 50 kilobytes. When you start exceeding 75 kilobytes, you may encounter deliverability problems.

The Pros and Cons of Text Emails

Text-only emails are not as elaborate as their HTML counterparts, nor are they perceived by marketers as glamorous, but they may indeed suit your purposes very well. If your audience wants quick access to important information, such as breaking news, legal briefs or research data, it is often in your best interest to use a text format. Such material forwards in a clean manner and is more easily readable on wireless and small screen devices than HTML email.

Text messages are easy to create since there are no graphics or other design elements, so they require no complex programming. The cost is minimal, and the message can reach all email clients. What's more, surveys show that one-third of email readers prefer text. The preference is even higher in some market segments, such as information technology and healthcare. If research and testing prove that this is true of your target market, focus on the quality of the content and go with a text version of your email. At a minimum, consider offering a text alternative to your HTML email and test each to see how customers respond.

Optimizing text-only emails

In text-only emails, you can't show product images or encourage action with buttons or enticing graphics. Don't expect your text message to do the same heavy lifting that your HTML messages do. What's more, you can't track open or forwarding rates, and some key features you identify with graphics in HTML won't be as obvious in text.

Follow these guidelines for creating your text template:

- **Use clear branding.** Since you can't use logos or colors, use the "From" address and subject line to identify yourself clearly.
- **Watch long URLs.** Use short URLs, even if you have to get your IT department or service provider to use post-click redirects in order to maintain your tracking metrics. Don't put URLs in mid-copy, even if that means you have to reword the basic message.
- **Move boilerplate info to the bottom.** Always lead with your top story or offer. Don't waste space at the top of the email with copy that never changes from one message to the next, such as who you are, why you sent the email and how readers can unsubscribe.
- **Use plenty of white space.** Make sure you place visual breaks between and around blocks of copy. These help to highlight offers and other key details while breaking up potentially eye-numbing blocks of text.
- **Limit line length.** Most email clients truncate the line at sixty characters, so use that as your metric. Always use hard breaks at the end of each line to preserve proper sentence breaks, because you can't count on auto-wrapping.
- **Limit paragraph length to four lines or fewer.** This aids onscreen readability. Make sure to have a blank line between paragraphs
- **Don't use punctuation marks or symbols for emphasis.** Spam filters watch out for garish punctuation marks, such as multiple exclamation points and other symbols that denote excitement. These will often cause your email to be blocked.
- **Use a fixed-space typeface.** This is one of the only ways to help achieve a consistent look among viewing windows. We usually suggest 10-point Courier or Courier New, both of which are easy to read.

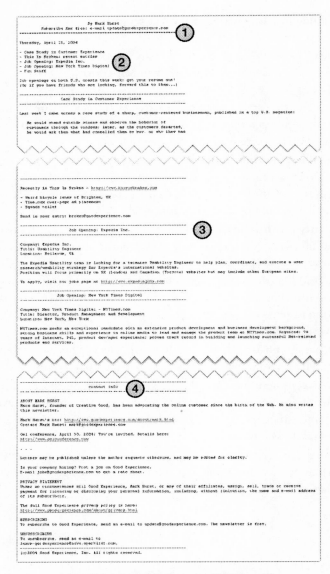

Good Experience's email newsletter has all the elements you would find in HTML, only in a format that is friendly for text. There is a header (1), a clear table of contents (2), white space to delineate between stories and improve readability (3) and, of course, a footer packed with important information that should not interfere with the main messages (4).

Text or HTML? Deciding Which Is Best for Your Program

According to a 2004 report by Jupiter Research, nearly 60% of email users have the ability to receive HTML emails. Such emails earn twice the response of text emails—an impressive feat! Take advantage of this opportunity, but still give your subscribers a choice. By offering both HTML and text versions, you allow customers to select what works best for them—a courtesy that does more to boost response and interest than any other relationship builder.

You can also make use of multi-part messaging (sometimes referred to as MIME) technology, which essentially enables you to send every recipient a single email that includes all of the available content-type versions, letting the recipient's email software figure out what to display. For example, you might send a text version, an HTML version, and even an AOL version. The email client renders the highest supported version. So, Outlook would render the HTML content, and a portable device might render the text content.

The advantage is that the recipient doesn't have to know whether they can accept HTML. But this can lead to fuzzy metrics. Talk to your IT folks or your ESP to find out exactly what is going to work for your program and how to use this technology to its maximum effect.

Another word of caution: Don't believe your IT folks if they tell you that you don't need to create a text version, because "the software will take care of it." Automatic programs are famous for mangling HTML emails when turning them into text—leaving a shell of their intended look and feel. Always create a text version using the principles outlined in this chapter.

Who Should Design Your Newsletter?

We can't overstate the importance of having a professional graphic designer handle this assignment. These professionals are trained to create layouts that are not only attractive but actually help the reader to navigate your content quickly and easily.

There may already be a designer on staff in your marketing department, but make sure that this person has experience in designing email and other online documents and newsletters, a significantly different media than print or even HTML web design.

The best option: A freelance designer

As with newsletter copywriting, your best option may be a freelancer graphic designer. Find a freelance designer who is an expert at designing for the online world, and email in particular. Nowadays, there are plenty to be found. Best of all, a good online designer will often do his or her own HTML programming, or be able to interface seamlessly with your tech team to make sure that the newsletter looks and functions the way it should.

As with a freelance writer, it's best to use only one designer for either the whole program, or for at least each newsletter, so that look and feel of your newsletter is consistent. A wise tactic is to have one designer create a variety of newsletter templates that are similarly attractive and effective. This way, you can use multiple designers if your workload demands it, and all of your newsletters will boast the same look and feel.

To find a good freelance designer, ask for references from your PR and marketing departments, or go online and check some of the many posting boards that advertise the services of these professionals.

Part I: Content Strategies Summary

- People will gladly accept advertising in exchange for information and entertainment, so the creation of a content-filled email newsletter is the best strategy to deliver your advertising messages to your audience with success.

- You can place sales messages throughout your newsletter, provided you do so tastefully. In fact, relevant content that your audience wants to read may be more effective at driving sales and response than pure promotional copy.

- A comprehensive program will include other non-newsletter emails, including event invitations, shipping and order confirmations and account information.

- Start with a general newsletter then offer several other, more specific newsletters that target specific segments of your audience.

- Only write about relevant, interesting subjects. Your audience will stick with you—and digest your sales messages—as long as you keep up your end of the bargain. This means that some marketing and executive "pet peeve" messages need to stay out.

- Make sure your email looks good on various email programs and monitors, including laptops and handhelds.

- Create fun or interesting emails that your subscribers will want to share with friends. This type of viral marketing is critical to keeping subscribers happy and building your subscriber base.

PART II

List Strategies

As with any other direct-marketing medium, your list is one of your top three critical success factors, along with creative and product offering. Even the most compelling message will be useless if it doesn't get to the people who are most likely to be interested in your information and act on your messages.

One of the great benefits of email is that it is more direct and interactive than traditional direct mail. In today's society, an increasing number of people are addicted to email, checking it religiously (almost compulsively) throughout the day. In fact, email is so pervasive in today's society that portable email devices are becoming nearly as common as cell phones, enabling millions of people to check their email without being anywhere near their computers. So while traditional mail, or "snail mail," only touches people once a day, in their mailboxes, email touches people throughout the day, right where they live, work and play.

Your list is such a critical part of an effective email newsletter campaign. This section covers the two critical steps that deal with building and maintaining your email list:

Chapter 4: Building a Large—and Responsive—Email List
Chapter 5: Keeping Your List Clean and Well Maintained

Chapter 4: Building a Large—and Responsive—Email List

Making email capture a priority has resulted in a remarkable turnaround in our email subscription numbers. After more than a year of steady decline, we were able to turn that trend around by adding sign-up forms on all of our pages, encouraging sign-ups during trial registration and including sign-up forms in the emails themselves. Together, these measures led to a 5% increase in our list size in little over a month—and it continues to grow every month.

—Chris Kilbourne, senior managing editor,
Business & Legal Reports

"The List." It's an element that is so important to any direct marketing campaign that it always brings out a heightened level of concern among marketers. How do I build a list? How much will it cost? How long will it take? Is my list growing? How fast? How does that compare to the industry? How can I grow my list faster? Why don't all my customers give me their email addresses? How can I get their email addresses if they don't give them to me themselves?

Relax. There are some proven methods for creating and growing lists. By implementing the methods that work best for your audience, you'll begin to build the type of list that makes the most sense for your business objectives. As you think about your list, remember two fundamental principles:

1. People will only provide their email address to companies they trust, and with the agreement that they will receive only what is promised.
2. If you don't get permission and honor it, your list will stop growing.

Always remember the number-one rule in email marketing: Never send an email without the permission of the person to whom it is being sent. This is spam. The only effective brand-building means of email marketing is by permission.

How to Get Permission

Permission to send emails to a consumer needs to be proactive and voluntary. The only correct way to get permission is to have people sign up with the understanding that they want to receive email from you.

The five levels of permission, from worst to best for consumers:

1. **Opt-out**: You obtain an email address for a consumer (it doesn't matter how) and begin emailing that consumer, allowing him to email or click to opt out of future mailings from you. Obviously, you can end up with huge amounts of subscribers this way—and there are ways to be an opt-out mailer and still be CAN-SPAM compliant—but this is the lowest form of permission, since one could argue it doesn't actually involve permission! While opt-out mailings will certainly drive some sales, in almost all circumstances we think it is too close to spam to be advisable.

2. **Negative Opt-in**: Here, you offer consumers an email subscription form, usually as part of an order form of some other kind, and you place a pre-checked box for an agreement to receive emails. The person must uncheck it in order not to receive the newsletter. Negative opt-in will get you more subscribers, but it may also leave you with more angry customers who don't realize they "agreed" to receive emails from you, think they're being spammed, harbor bad feelings about your products and brand and usually unsubscribe in the end. Those who feel abused by this process are certainly not buying anything from you.

3. **Opt-in**: A subscriber must proactively check a box in order to receive your newsletter. Opt-in is the most common form of subscription, because it is voluntary on the part of the subscriber and it keeps things simple.

4. **Confirmed Opt-in**: A subscriber opts in to your newsletter and then receives an email message from you confirming their subscription and offering them the option to unsubscribe immediately if the subscription was in any way a mistake. This level of permission increases the value of

your list and protects you to some extent against charges of spamming. It also increases the deliverability of the list, since bad addresses will generate immediate bounces to the confirmation mailing and never get on the list.

5. **Double Opt-in** (sometimes referred to as "verified opt-in"): In this scenario, someone subscribes to your email list and then receives an email message from you to which they must reply in order to be on your list. This is the gold standard for permission, as consumers essentially have to subscribe to your list twice in order to get on it (meaning they really, really want your emails!). However, you do run the risk of losing subscribers who don't realize they need to send you another message to actually get on your list. You can take steps to minimize this risk by sending the confirmation email immediately and by messaging to the consumer on the web page following the subscription to remind him to go check his email and confirm, but we've never seen a double opt-in rate higher than 80% of subscribers, and many come in closer to 60%.

Which is best for your program?

We believe there is absolutely no reason to have anything less than a confirmed opt-in standard for your newsletter. In our experience, opt-out and negative opt-in lists, while large, perform poorly and generate complaints that lead to blocking and filtering. If you're going to have an opt-in list, there's no reason not to make it confirmed opt-in. The extra step will improve customer service and deliverability and prevent fraudulent subscriptions. (We'll talk more about sending welcome messages later.) Many mailers find that the higher hurdle of double opt-in is worth it in terms of producing an even more responsive list. We think whether confirmed opt-in or double opt-in is right for you depends on the kind of newsletter you have and what you're trying to achieve with it.

Thank you for your request.

Your confirmation is required. Simply click the link below
to confirm your recent PostMasterDirect information request.

http://c.pmd.bz/c?E=davidz%40netcreations.com&T=20040916038798434

If asked, your codes are E:davidz@netcreations.com T:20040916038798434.

Remember: You may remove yourself from this service or change the content
you receive at any time. To protect your privacy, we will not activate
your request until you confirm.

This service will be managed by our partner, PostMasterDirect, who will send you relevant offers from third parties.

PostMasterDirect's privacy policy can be viewed at: http://www.postmasterdirect.com/privacy.html

Once you confirm, you will be added to:
IT Professionals
surveys

We hope you enjoy the convenience and we'll see you online!

Thanks!
PostMasterDirect

Request received at: PostMasterDirect
Time of request: Thu Sep 16 15:38:29 2004 EST
IP address received: IP address received: 209.208.237.207
Email address received: davidz@netcreations.com

** ▓▓▓▓▓▓▓▓▓▓▓▓▓▓

PostMasterDirect, 379 West Broadway, Ste 202,
New York, NY 10012, 212-625-1370 x218

Double opt-in is the best way to ensure that the folks on your list really want to
be there. Once a user "opts in" to receive product information based on topical
categories of interest, a confirmation email is sent to her prompting her to
confirm her subscription. She simply clicks the confirmation link to complete
the process. Although you will lose some prospects (those who do not complete
the second step), you virtually guarantee that everyone on your list really wants
to be there. What a great forum for your content and promotions.

Ways to Build Your List

There are many ways to build a huge list of email addresses of people who are
interested in your company, its products or its services and are willing to give you
permission to send emails. These can be placed into two broad categories:

1. **Organic Capture**: Non-paid means to inspire people to provide their email addresses.
2. **Paid Acquisition**: Gaining addresses through advertising, list rental, partnerships, and more.

Leveraging Organic Capture to Build Your List

What could be better than building a good mailing list without having to put out critical marketing dollars? You'd be hard pressed to find a marketer who wouldn't be interested in a no-cost, yet high-quality, method of building an email list. This is the whole premise behind organic capture: using methods and mechanisms that you already have in place to create or grow your email address list. Sound too good to be true? It's not. Best of all, when you employ organic methods, you will almost definitely build a list that is more accurate and targeted than one you might rent or purchase. Even better, there are many ways to do it. We'll go over some of the most effective techniques we've seen, but as you read, you'll find that gathering emails organically should become more than an exercise—it should become a part of your marketing lifestyle.

Using Your Web Site to Build Your List

Making email collection a priority means giving it prominence throughout the design of your web site. A call to sign up for your newsletter must be prominent on every single page of your site. Remember that most visitors are there to browse through and learn more about your company and products. Entice these browsers to engage with your company. No one should leave your site without leaving behind his or her email address. The success of your site should be measured by its ability to capture emails, not just hits or sales.

Start with the homepage. A prompt or link encouraging the reader to sign up should be in the top half of the screen as well as in multiple locations throughout the page. If visitors have to scroll or search to find the sign-up form, you will earn a much lower capture rate. Take special care to craft a compelling offer—visibility is only half the battle. Your sign-up invitation must also entice and persuade.

But don't stop there. People may come to a page on your site through the side door, so to speak. Web searching is non-linear, meaning people will not always enter your site through the homepage. A search-engine link may land the reader on any of the pages on your site. They may never even see the homepage. Therefore, you must display prompts for email sign-up prominently on every page of your site. Even if you have a site that most users do read from top to bottom, having a sign-up form on every page is still important to make sure that at any time in a user's brief visit to your site, an email subscribe form is visible, or at least present on the page. A link to a "newsletter subscription" page doesn't do the job nearly as well as a live form on the page itself.

If you have several newsletters, you'll want to have specific calls to action that match content on your site with the topics of the newsletters. For example, the "Business & Technology" page at BarnesandNoble.com includes a very prominent subscription form on the left-hand sidebar for newsletters related to business and computers. One of our clients, Business & Legal Reports, created a mini-subscription form with specific newsletters for their interior pages. These quickly accounted for over 50% of their web sign-ups and increased their web to email conversion by 108%!

BLR demonstrates a way to gather email addresses using their web site. The benefits of joining and the content options are all well placed and easy to find (1). The prompt for the email address is obvious (2), as is the subscribe button (3).

Since email capture is the single most important aspect of your marketing campaign, keep tweaking the wording of your calls to action and the placement on the pages until you see optimal results, namely, a rapidly-growing email list.

In addition, provide an easy way for readers to forward all the goodies you offer via email (and encourage them to do so), including product specs, graphics, articles, statistics, surveys or any other material featured on your web site. For example:

- Next to that fabulous new pair of boots featured on your site, shoppers can click to "Tell a Friend about This Sale."
- Alongside an article about the latest in Mediterranean cuisine, readers can "Share Recipes with a Friend."
- Right below your bold and vibrant invitation announcement of a new gallery opening, readers can choose to "Invite a Friend to the Cultural Event of the Summer."

This is the same principle we covered in Chapter 1 about viral emails that people want to pass along to others. Always encourage readers to pass your web site content along via email, and always make sure those emails have at least a small pitch or even a live form so the recipient can subscribe to your regular newsletter program. After all, the more opportunities you present for organic capture, the greater the potential for positive results.

Designing Subscribe Forms That Encourage Sign-Up

In your efforts to collect email, don't put up data-collection obstacles. Every time you ask the reader to register, use a password, answer questions on a survey or provide personal data, you are essentially setting up roadblocks, each of which has the potential to make the would-be subscriber decide it's not worth the trouble. Just as ecommerce sites never put any barrier between the shopper and the sale, don't prioritize getting a lot of data over getting the one piece of information you need most: her email address!

You can always gather additional data later on using surveys and feedback forms, once you've opened the lines of communication (much more on this in Chapter 6), or by appending the data (which we cover later in this chapter). By asking only for the person's email address and permission to send them emails, you are keeping it simple and not driving away potential business.

There are two imperatives to creating an irresistible subscribe form:

1. **Provide a compelling reason to sign up.** This might be an incentive, such as a money-saving coupon, a free gift or perhaps a gift certificate for

another company with which you have a partnership. But whether you have an incentive or not, be sure that your form has strong promotional copy touting the benefits of receiving the newsletter.

2. **Design a super-fast sign-up process.** Do this in order to quickly capture the email address and only the most basic additional information (we recommend either just email or, at most, one additional field, like zip code or gender). Close while the prospect is hot.

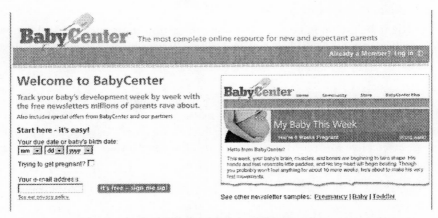

BabyCenter's homepage is designed to capture email addresses. In case the parent-friendly design and pleasant colors aren't enough, the viewer's eye is drawn to the incredibly simple sign-up process. Note that the only information required to sign up is the email address and your baby's due date or birthday (those who aren't parents yet can check the "Trying to get pregnant" box instead). Additional information is requested on a subsequent page, and additional newsletters are offered there as well. By minimizing required fields and making the email newsletter both prominent and enticing, BabyCenter enjoys a double-digit sign-up rate.

We worked with a major consumer packaged-goods company whose newsletter was well designed and filled with terrific content. In spite of these good qualities, they couldn't get anyone to sign up for the newsletter. When we dug into it, we discovered the subscribe form had seventeen required fields! We weren't surprised that most consumers weren't willing to go through all of that work just to get email, even if it was from a brand-name marketer. We advised that they just ask for the email address up front. Within weeks of making the change their sign-up rate skyrocketed, at one point hitting a high of 400% improvement!

As we mentioned earlier, you can always gather more data later, once you have built up a relationship based on trust. For example, when a prospect requests a download of your latest whitepaper, ask for their email address and include a checkbox to subscribe to your newsletter. Later, when the prospect responds with interest in a product demo, you might ask for telephone number, company name and job title. The prospect will be much more likely to provide this information when they have learned more about your company.

One way to entice people to give you more data is to offer an incentive. This works particularly well when the data and incentive are tied together. Remember the marketer with the seventeen fields? Well, what they really wanted was their customers' mailing addresses. Our suggestion was to offer the incentive of a $1 coupon that would come in the mail. How did it work? For starters, this eliminated the garbage-data problem, because if you didn't give the correct address, you wouldn't get the coupon. And while not everyone who signed up for email filled in this second form, many others did. In fact, the postal data supplied under the new offering was much more accurate.

Therefore, always think about why you want a certain piece of data and how you intend to use it. If, for example, you want to do geographical target marketing, but not actually send anything by mail, then ask only for their area code, zip code, or state. This allows you to target an area for marketing purposes without requiring a high level of trust, since the data is not personally identifiable.

Surveys are also good ways to acquire additional information. People love to share their opinions, and you can often sneak a few demographic questions in at the same time.

Finally, don't fall into the trap of gathering information just for the sake of it. If you have no reason to be gathering data at this time, don't ask for it. Remember, the more data you own, the more privacy issues you have to contend with. In today's climate, if you don't really need it or intend to use it, you might not want it.

Asking for Emails in the Real World

Think of your offline customer touch points in the same way you do your web site—every point is an opportunity to gather email addresses. Of course, you'll want to ask in a way that reassures customers that their privacy will be upheld, and you'll also want to offer a compelling benefit statement.

Asking for email addresses in retail stores

People will give you email at retail if you ask respectfully and make the benefits clear. But it takes more than index cards scattered throughout the store.

You'll need to:

- **Provide a compelling reason.** For example: "Sign up at this store to receive email and our manager will personally notify you when there are special sales here (and we'll tell you first)!" The purpose is to give a concrete reason that erases the suspicion that you are going to send spam.

- **Make it painless.** The sign-up form should be no more than a small piece of paper that goes into a drop-box while they are waiting in line. Or, allow them to provide it to the store associate and have it entered into the computer.

- **Use a focused incentive.** Offer something that makes it worth their while, such as a discount coupon or store credit, but don't give away something that is tempting to non-buyers, like a cash prize. The best example of this was a high-end men's shoe store that offered a bottle of shoe polish in exchange for an email address and permission. That's an incentive that is only interesting to the target audience—men who buy quality shoes.

- **Reassure them.** Mention multiple times that the email will be used only for specific offers and that they can unsubscribe at any time.

- **Get the staff into the act.** There are some tricks to deal with data entry and to motivate staff. Some of our clients have offered the clerks an incentive or commission for every email they capture and enter into the database. Others have sent emails designed to be printed and redeemed for discounts in the store. The store staff can see how email effectively drives store traffic. Store managers, who may see the web site as a threat to their business, will be less resistant to collecting emails and will gain an understanding of how email can boost in-store sales. Once you get the managers on board, they will apply their own creative energy. One of our best experiences was when a waitress, arriving with the check after a pleasant meal, invited us to join the email list so we could earn free desserts. Of course we signed up right away! It worked, because the timing was perfect, the offer was sweet (literally) and our server had already built up a level of trust with us.

REI does a terrific job of using email newsletters to promote in-store activities. A bold headline (1) identifies the audience and lets them know that there are timely and exciting events happening at their local REI store. Readers can quickly scan the convenient list (2) of events and click to read more about those of interest.

Trade shows and other live events

Every booth at every trade show on the planet has a fishbowl or some other container designed to gather business cards. The whole point of trade shows is to meet lots of people in your market and get their information so you can continue the conversation after the show.

You can use a lot of the same methods here that you would use to capture email in retail stores; however, since trade show attendees are always looking to win something or get something for free, an incentive, such as a prize, usually works best. The trick is to balance volume with quality. This begins with choosing trade shows that are likely to have high-quality prospects. But beyond that, you can further segment the crowd by offering several newsletter checkboxes on the sign-up card. Also, take care in choosing your prize. Everyone is going to sign up to win the hot consumer gadget of the week. That's probably not helpful. Instead, identify the prize that will quicken the pulse of your target prospects—and be completely uninteresting to everyone else. And of course, have a sign posted that clearly states that the business card in your fishbowl serves as permission to send them email!

Call center, direct mail, advertising and more

Operators working in your call center should be asking for email as part of their call center script. There should be a short benefit statement to read that lets people know why they should sign up. Also, the operators need to be trained to take down an email address with the proper format. Alert your customers to watch for a welcome email within a few hours (or the fastest timeframe you can manage). The first email should reference the fact that the customer was signed up via the call center.

Direct mail, including catalogs, should also have a call to action, asking people for their email and explaining the benefits they will receive from your newsletter, such as great shopping tips or inside information on the hottest new home-decorating trends. In fact, anything you send to customers or prospects by mail, including products and promotional items, should include a card that promotes your newsletters and asks for their email address.

Using Forward to a Friend (FTAF) in Email

As we discussed in Chapter 1, viral marketing is a terrific way to get your content distributed to an even wider audience and ultimately built your list. After all, what could be better than having your customers do your marketing for you? It's an idea that has been around for a long time: word-of-mouth. It is a primary factor in keeping books on the bestseller list, restaurants crowded on a nightly basis and movies popular long after the initial box-office blitz.

Email is ideally suited for this type of information sharing, since the forward button is a standard part of all email software programs. One look at your own inbox should be enough to convince you that people know how to forward. So use it to your advantage. But don't trust that it will happen without some encouragement. Always include links or forms in your email message that encourage subscribers to forward your email to any friends who might appreciate the information.

One reason is psychological. Seeing the word "forward" will induce people to do so. In fact, just including the word, without any fancy forms or links, will increase your chances of someone hitting the forward button. For example, MarketingSherpa always includes the notation "Pls Forward" at the end of every subject line.

More importantly, you can better track viral behavior if readers use the tools you provide rather than hitting their program's forward button. You also have more control over the message that the recipient gets with a system designed for that purpose. It's worth your time to make your forwarding tools easy to use.

So, don't stop with just a link. While a link will encourage forwarding, an even more effective way to do so is to embed a form in the email. On it, you can have the pre-filled name and email address of the sender and include an open box where he or she can put the names of friends along with their email addresses. It makes the whole process faster, easier and much cooler.

As with all email, you want to make sure your messages look good when forwarded to different size monitors and handheld devices, so be sure to check for broken text or graphics and make sure that the entire message, including all instructions, are visible and easy to read.

Consider This: Content Is Part of Your List-Building Strategy

If a reader sees an ad for a DVD player and knows that one of his friends is looking to buy one, he might forward the ad to his pal. If, however, this same reader gets a trailer and a review of the hottest new DVD release, accompanied by the same ad for the DVD player, he will be more likely to forward the trailer (and the ad) to ten of his friends whom he knows will want to see it. That's because interesting, innovative content always gets forwarded and thus reaches more people. In our example, several of those ten people may be looking for a new DVD player, thus increasing your chances of making a sale.

Creating a Forward-to-a-Friend Form

A successful FTAF form is one that successfully delivers on your invitation or call to action.

From a functional perspective, FTAF forms should allow you to control the data flow, collect some additional data on your customers, insert marketing messages and encourage the people receiving the email to opt in for your newsletters. Keep the form short and easy to navigate. Also, prominently display your privacy and spam policy on the form—make it clear that you will not send other emails to their friends unless they explicitly subscribe.

Make it obvious and easy

Place the call to action for your FTAF in an obvious place right up top, as well as in several other locations, including in the footer. Set the form up so that readers can easily enter the names of friends without having to think about it too much. The more work, the less likely they are to forward.

The more the merrier

Why stop at one friend? Typically, if you provide several boxes for signing up several friends, the sender will do just that. They may not include friends on every line, but they will likely list two or three people. Set it up so that friends will be listed in separate form fields and include subscription information for each friend. Try providing a different number of address lines to find out how many friends most people are comfortable forwarding to. You can even have some programming done to create cookies that automatically repopulate future forms with the addresses from previous forwards!

Allow people to personalize it

When someone forwards a great email to a friend, they will usually want to put their personal stamp on it by adding something such as, "This reminded me of our conversation this morning" or "I thought of you when I saw this." For this reason, you'll want to leave a space where the sender can write her own personal message. In addition, you want the email to appear as though it is coming from the sender (the "From" line) and not from your company, so that it is more welcomed and won't be misconstrued as spam.

DailyCandy has a really well-designed FTAF form. It allows you to send to several friends without having to use commas (1), it offers a reassuring privacy statement (2) and it lets you write a nice note to your friend (3).

Getting Friends to Subscribe

Once someone has signed up for your newsletter and then forwarded it to his friends, you need to get the friends' explicit permission to send them your regular newsletter emails. You can close this loop if you construct your regular emails with the non-subscriber also in mind.

Therefore, make sure that every forwarded email features a way for the receiver to subscribe. Make the subscribe instructions clear and have them lead directly to a simple sign-up form on which email address is the only "required" data field. DailyCandy.com, a fashion site, uses a simple, fun and effective call to action that asks: "Did a friend send you this? From now on, be the first to find out. Sign up for DailyCandy. It's fun, it's pretty and it's free." It's a clearly worded, strong promotion that makes sense for their audience and their content.

This email offers an example of viral marketing mechanics in action. It has an enticing call to action to forward to your friends (1) and encourages these friends to sign up for their own copy (2).

Using Cross-Promotion Opportunities

To maximize your marketing possibilities, always mention your other newsletters in each mailing. Every email and every subscribe form should cross-promote all other email newsletters you publish. This gives each reader options. If, for example, someone receives your email newsletter about the latest shoe fashions, forwarded from a friend, they may like it enough to sign up for your emails, which will put information about your shoe line in front of them every week. However, if given the opportunity to read about great ways to accessorize as well, they might also sign up for your other newsletter on accessorizing tips. This builds your list and deepens your relationships with subscribers.

Asking for Emails in Non-Marketing Emails

Take advantage of every email communication that your company has with a customer or prospect to encourage them to sign up for your newsletter. Many companies don't do this, missing out on a huge opportunity to build their lists easily and effectively.

Use every other email that you send in the normal course of business. Any time you send an email you should include information about your email newsletters. This includes customer-service auto-replies, order confirmations, shipping notifications and account-management messages. If someone makes a purchase from you, they are expecting to get notifications by email that their order was received or that it has been shipped. You can easily include a few well-placed and relevant marketing messages for your newsletters and other email offers.

Also, think about how many individual emails you and your employees send out each day to partners, customers, vendors and prospects. Depending on the size of your company, it could be hundreds, if not thousands. Each person receiving one of these emails already has a reason to be communicating with you, so they should be receiving your newsletter.

Create a templated block of copy that promotes your newsletter and provides subscription instructions. Then have each employee in your company insert this information at the bottom of their signature file. That's it.

Turn Transaction Emails into Selling Opportunities

The merging of CRM and marketing is happening online faster and more deeply than ever before. Any company that sends bills by postal mail long ago learned billing statement stuffers generate better response than other direct mail. Use that same tactic online to build your email database, connect with customers more frequently and sell additional services.

Airlines were among the first to apply this technique to email. American Airlines, United and others regularly send frequent-flier mile updates that always include promotions for trips. More recently, Apple's iTunes service has leveraged its email "receipts" to try and upsell songs or albums that purchasers might like, based on their past purchases. Of course, there's also eBay, a pioneer in all kinds of interactive marketing practices. Their emails notifying members of winning bids are a well-balanced mix of necessary information, content, marketing and branding.

It makes sense to encourage consumers to manage their accounts online and to ask them permission to send them shipping, transaction and billing information via email. This will be far more appealing to a greater number of customers than "special offers by email." However, you can use these emails for any number of "soft" promotional links intended to up sell and cross-sell.

Moreover, transactional messages give you another legitimate reason to be in the inbox on a regular basis, increasing your opportunities to create brand awareness. These messages are also more likely to get whitelisted by recipients and less likely to be blocked by ISPs.

To maintain strong relationships, do not restrict customers to one choice or the other. Allow them to receive account information via snail mail, email or both. Don't penalize customers for selecting one over the other. The key is to not coerce customers into getting these messages, but to make them want them.

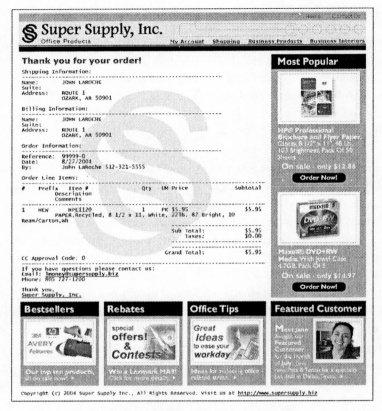

Non-marketing emails can be powerful promotional tools, so don't ignore them. This example proves that even routine transaction messages, such as shipping confirmations, can be cool, exciting and enticing. This simulation was created by Message Effect, Inc., a company that helps clients customize transactional messages by providing a targeted mix of promotions for add-on products as well as branding messages.

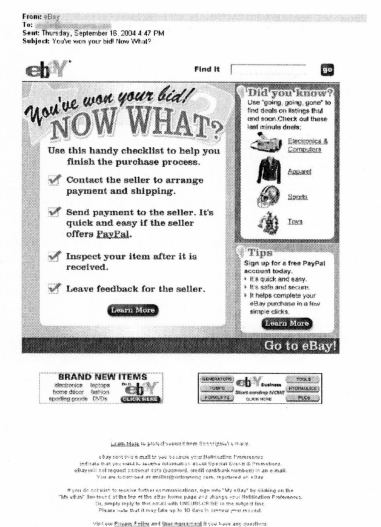

Transactional messages aren't limited to shipping confirmations, as seen in this example from eBay. This system message sent to an auction winner includes a well-balanced mix of necessary information, content, marketing and branding.

Create an Affiliate Program That People Want to Join.

Nothing motivates people to take action more than "making it worth their while." That's why a terrific method for gathering email referrals is to turn your email program into an affiliate program, where subscribers who refer others to your site get credit for sales. You can do this easily, by first setting up a separate tracking code for your own email messages that allows you to track how recipients behave and then assigning credit, even if the visitor comes back later, enters through a different channel and so on. You can also assign a revenue share to email-driven purchases for budgeting purposes.

Consider This: Organic Capture Methods Demand Sound Business Principles

There's an old saying in advertising that declares, "A good campaign will put a bad company out of business faster." This is important to remember when employing organic forms of marketing, because viral marketing is a sword that can cut both ways. Just as good business practices will garner you excellent credibility, lack of quality will ruin you. And because of the speed of email and the community environment of the internet, the news of a bad experience will spread much more rapidly than news of a good experience. A strong viral email program makes it even more critical that you have a well-tested and reliable product, strong customer service and the desire to satisfy every customer.

Using Paid Acquisition to Grow Your List

No matter what business you are in, you are probably not reaching every available prospect. Additionally, as your business evolves and you develop new product lines and features, you will want to get the word out to new target markets. Just as smart marketing—including online and offline advertising and promotions— will drive customers to your web site, toll-free number and retail locations, you can also use paid advertising methods to build your email house file.

There are several proven methods to build your list using paid sources in a quick and cost-effective manner. If this is the way you choose to go, be sure never to work with anyone who is willing to hand you a list. Such a list is likely to be a spam list. There are several trustworthy ways to rent a high-quality list, and each offers its own set of advantages and disadvantages.

This conceptual example shows how a toy company could use a list rental acquisition campaign to drive sign-up for its newsletter program. While Acme Toys could certainly have made this email an ad for its products, and gained some new sales, in the long-run it will drive more revenue with this approach. Why? Because signing up for an email newsletter is much easier than whipping out a credit card and buying a product—especially from a company you may not be familiar with. By getting more new people to sign up for the email, Acme Toys can use relevant content to form a strong relationship, which also provides the ability to promote its products and build trust. This technique is even more effective because the newsletter being offered is compelling to the target audience.

Renting or Buying a List

List rental is a huge component of most offline direct-marketing plans. Nothing can surpass it in terms of targeting and control of content. Similarly, a good email list can provide a valuable source of qualified prospects. After all, you already know something extremely important about them: they have opted in to an email list and are therefore comfortable with the email channel.

However, email list rental can be risky business. There are a number of list brokers who sell lists they have gathered by what can be best described as questionable practices. Some lists are outright stolen. And if you mail to a spam list, even inadvertently, you will be seen as a spammer, which will destroy your credibility not only with customers but with the ISPs and the email industry, and which may impact your ability to send email successfully for years to come.

That said, there are several reputable companies that get explicit permission to send emails from companies like yours. They will never sell you a list, but they will send your email promotion to their list. (See the sidebar "Vetting Data Partners" later in this chapter for details on how to tell the good guys from the bad guys.) There are two ways this works:

Third-party offers

Publishers, such as the *New York Times* or iVillage, collect millions of email addresses from consumers to send them newsletters and other content. At the same time, they will ask, and often get, permission to send third-party messages. When the subscriber opts in, they are granting the publisher permission to send them emails from third parties, such as your business. The email that the consumer gets will have a "From" address, header and footer from the company that holds the permission. But the rest of the message will be your ad. Your goal is to develop an ad that is so engaging and compelling it will drive folks to visit your web site or sign up for your email newsletter in droves.

With the right partner, this can be a great way to reach a large audience that is willing to look at what you are sending. Of course, like all other types of advertising, the success of this tactic is only as good as your offer, copy, design and so forth. Take time to analyze the audience, considering what makes sense to put in front of them and so on. Plan the way you would for any other media campaign. A third-party email promotion requires the same planning as other forms of advertising.

Traditional list rental

There are also companies that gather email addresses for the express purpose of sending offers from other companies. Again, be careful who you work with, as sometimes subscribers have joined a list in exchange for some kind of incentive, like a chance to win a prize, and not because they are really interested in or qualified to respond to offers from companies like yours. The email that is sent through these services have your "From" address, header and footer. It should also include information about the service where the subscriber opted in—either above your header, below your footer or both. While the email looks like it comes from your company, you do not actually get the list, but instead you send your creative to the partner, who then pushes the send button. This also means you have no control over the deliverability of the message. You should ask the vendor about their deliverability rates to make sure that your messages are making it to the prospects. You will find more detail on deliverability in Chapter 8.

Consider This: Why You Need to Make Friends with a Good List Broker

Of course you know that if you want to do paid acquisition you need a good list broker to help you buy reputable lists only. But you can also consider hiring a reputable list manager who can work with you to build a separate third-party-offers list and monetize it for you. The revenue will offset your newsletter costs. This is common in both the offline and online world.

Advertising for Your List

A good way to build your list is to actually run ads that encourage people to sign up for your newsletter. It's no different than how any magazine or newspaper advertises subscriptions to their publication. This can be a wise move, since the initial investment of marketing dollars can increase your ability to communicate more cost efficiently by email and give you many more opportunities to sell to people who subscribe.

This is an easier case to make with online advertising, since, in addition to being more affordable than other media, it speaks only to people who are online—your prime targets to receive and read email.

Along this same idea, be sure to promote your newsletter in all offline forms of advertising, whether in print, direct mail or even broadcast form. If you're spending money on promoting your company, be sure that it encourages sign-up to your email program. In the long run, you'll be converting prospects to a much more affordable method of marketing.

Strategic Partnerships That Build Lists

You can build your list quickly through the use of strategic partnerships. Look for companies who target similar demographic audiences with their web sites and emails, but who are not your direct competitors.

You can then strike up any of several means of partnerships:

- **Barter ads**: This highly effective means of growing your email list can include exchanges of email newsletter ads with another company or placement of ads on each other's web pages.
- **Co-registration deals**: This is an effective practice for sites that are targeting a similar audience with non-competing products or services. In this case, you add an option to sign up for the other company's email newsletter on your site and they include an option to sign up for your newsletter on their site. For example, take two sites that target men, age twenty to thirty. The first focuses on the latest sports news. The second promotes deals on male exercise and fitness. When men are signing up to receive the newsletter from the sports news site, they are asked if they are interested in receiving a newsletter from the fitness site, and vice versa.
- **Affiliate programs**: Here you are paying the other web site for sending you subscribers. The ad runs for free on the affiliate's web page, and when someone signs up for your newsletter through that source, you pay the affiliate. It's important that you calculate the value of each new subscriber, or the cost of conversion, so that you can accurately determine a fair per-address price.
- **Syndication**: Spread your content around. If your content is truly unique and valuable, you can use it to leverage and build your list and your brand by syndicating the material to other newsletters. If, for example, your newsletter is for a dance site and you know of a newsletter for the site of a theater company, you may, as non-competing artistic associations, share the content and run each other's articles. In addition, you will want to include sign-up options for each other's newsletters, as outlined in the co-registration section above. This is a way to gain additional quality content and to build your list by introducing your newsletter information to the readers of another newsletter.

- **Co-branding products and newsletters**: If your company is known for quality content, you can try partnering up with another company that specializes in a product. Offer to give them an existing newsletter, or perhaps create a new one that suits their interests and gives them sole sponsorship. By providing quality content you will grow your list, while the sponsor can benefit from the opportunity to market their product(s) to a growing audience.

Before entering into any kind of partnership deals, due diligence is required on your part. If the company you are looking to align with has a reputation for sending spam (and some well-known companies are spammers), you will become a spammer by association. Also be aware of the overall reputation of any company with which you strike a deal. Many businesses have lost customers by choosing the wrong partners.

Lessons from the Inbox:
Vetting Data Partners (or, Making Sure Your Partners are on the Up-And-Up)

Be very careful with whom you work and especially with partners who send email that looks like it comes from you. Your brand reputation is on the line, and the last thing you want is for anyone receiving your emails to feel that they are being spammed. That's why it is critical that all potential partners are vetted, or thoroughly examined, to ensure that their business practices mirror your own.

When considering a list rental company, you must ensure that the email addresses on the list are permission based, deliverable and free of spam-traps (fake email addresses created to identify and snare spammers who accumulate their lists by harvesting email address from web sites). Make sure that the process your potential data partner has used to acquire email addresses meets your standards. This includes checking the registration process to make sure it is clear to the subscriber exactly what they are signing up for. The privacy policy must be clear and easy to locate, and it must match your intentions for use of the list.

A confirmation to verify the email address and gain permission should also be in place. Validated lists, ones where the subscriber must confirm that they want to be on the list by clicking on a link or taking some other action, is the preferred permission standard for list rental. Check to see that the unsubscribe process is simple and that requests are processed correctly and quickly. Finally, you must make sure your partners are complying with federal and all appropriate state anti-spam legislation.

To make things clear and simple, use this checklist for evaluating data partners:

Check web sites' registration source for:

- A clear opt-in process
- High email verification/permission level
- Strict adherence to privacy policy
- Working unsubscribe methods or pages
- Proper use of collected email addresses

Check the reputation of sites by

- Asking for references
- Conducting an IP search via SpamCop
- Scanning Google Groups for complaints
- Checking DNS Stuff for blacklist, IP info and abuse.net use

When renting lists, also

- Check deliverability at key ISPs
- Monitor for spam-trap address inclusion
- Verify CAN-SPAM compliance of emails sent
- Quarantine emails collected until tested and conduct periodic reputation audits

Appending Information to Your Existing Customer Records

You can easily gather additional information on customers—for a fee—by appending data to your list. That means buying additional information from a reputable database marketing company, such as Experian, Acxiom or InfoUSA. The practice of appending customer information is a hot topic these days, because it is an easy way to learn lots of detailed information about your customers, so we'll cover the key issues and, of course, alert you to the potential pitfalls.

Appending email and postal addresses

If you have a file of postal addresses without corresponding email addresses, a database marketing company can easily supply you with this information. Additionally, if you have a business email address, a database marketing company may be able to supply you with their personal email address, or vice versa. The advantage of appending is that it can help you grow your list quickly with people who have, at some point, contacted you or been a customer. The disadvantage is that it raises serious permission issues, since the person did not give you their email address directly. If you do anger people on this list, they may include some of your best customers! So be cautious, and work only with companies that take care to communicate with the email recipients about how their email address is going to be used and shared.

In addition, whenever you use this method to gain someone's email address, it is always a good idea send a welcome message that lets them know why they turned up on your list and that clearly demonstrates why they will want to remain on the list. Some sort of incentive might also be in order.

Appending demographic data

By using the email addresses, postal addresses or other information that you have already gathered, a database marketing company can also provide you with a considerable amount of demographic data. The key elements can include age, gender, race, income and other key information to help you better understand your customers and segment your lists for targeting purposes. This process is less problematic than getting actual addresses, since it is mainly invisible to the consumer, but you can raise their ire if they realize you have information they did not provide to you.

Use caution when appending data

The practice of appending your data is perfectly legal, but it does raise permission issues. In fact, the Direct Marketing Association (DMA) has even issued a new section in its *Guidelines for Ethical Business Practice* that deals with email append. The DMA outlines a variety of important points on this issue, the most important being that a marketer should append a consumer's email address to its database only when the consumer gives the marketer permission to add his or her email address to their database or if there is an established business relationship with that consumer, either online or offline. Additionally, the DMA states that the data used in the append process should be from sources that provided notice and choice regarding the acceptance of third-party email offers and where the consumer did not "opt out." For more information on DMA guidelines, go to the DMA website (www.the-dma.org).

Bottom line: Be sure you don't violate any agreements that you have with subscribers. If your subscribers realize that you have information about them that they did not provide, they will very likely unsubscribe—and may even stop doing business with you altogether.

Also keep in mind that you get what you pay for, so you'll pay more money for more detailed—and higher quality—information. Data gets old very quickly. So, if you do spend the money to gather such information, it is to your advantage to use it quickly before email addresses change and other data becomes obsolete.

Our philosophy is that the data you collect from eager customers is always far better than data that you buy, because voluntary information is more reliable, more accurate and more up-to-date. Plus, it has the "stamp of approval" of the participant. It may also be cheaper, even factoring in the cost of any incentives or promotions. However, appending data can quickly and easily provide you with information that would be extremely difficult, if not impossible, to get any other way.

Chapter 5: Keeping Your List Clean and Well Maintained

It's not the most glamorous aspect of email marketing, but there is no question that list hygiene is essential for maintaining the success of your efforts. Having a large percentage of bad or outdated addresses in your database wastes time, money and bandwidth. Sending to email addresses that don't exist pegs you as a spammer in the eyes of the ISP servers. Content, design and customer segmentation end up taking the blame for declining metrics when the real problem could be the list.

—Angela Caltagirone, direct marketing services
manager/EDM, Williams-Sonoma Inc.

Since your email newsletter program creates and sustains a long-term relationship with your subscribers, assembling the list the first time is by no means the end of the task. Constant efforts must be made to make sure that your list, or lists, are well maintained. That includes everything from making sure that the addresses are always current and valid to knowing how to handle a request to unsubscribe. How you handle each situation will play a critical role in how your subscribers view your organization and how effective your email program will be in the long term.

How to Handle Unsubscribes

Don't take it personally when someone requests to no longer receive your newsletter. This request to unsubscribe is not a rejection of your company. It may not even be a rejection of your email. And there could be dozens of reasons why, many of which have nothing to do with what you send. People simply grow tired of a topic or no longer fit your target audience.

For example, the parent of a child who has "left the nest" may no longer need your newsletter on raising children, or an executive who has been transferred from New York City to Miami may no longer wish to receive your weekly newsletter on "Things to Do in Manhattan." Whatever the reason, this is a make-or-break moment for the relationship, because these are still potential customers, depending, of course, on how you handle the requests.

Unsubscribe management best practices

- **Make it instant:** Your unsubscribe process should be instantaneous and 100% successful. No exceptions. What's more, the request to unsubscribe must always be processed immediately. Delays, even of as little as two days, are never acceptable in the eyes of users, although delays of up to ten days are permissible under CAN-SPAM. If you send a second mailing to someone who already unsubscribed because you haven't processed the request yet, you've just acted like a spammer and lost all of your hard-earned credibility.

- **Make it clear and easy:** The only acceptable method of handling unsubscribe requests is "click to unsubscribe" or the equivalent. Don't require passwords, account numbers or log-ins to unsubscribe; you don't need that information to remove them from your list, so don't ask for it. And don't obscure the links to your unsubscribe page. You're only making these folks jump through unnecessary hoops that will cause them irritation. If they want off the list, let them off the list. It doesn't help your response and success metrics to "pad" your list with folks who are not interested. They will simply delete your emails unread, put your company on their personal block list or, worse yet, complain to their ISP, which may block your future mailings to all of its customers. All your success metrics depend on having a clean list of interested people so that when you track response you are doing so from a solid base. Otherwise, you'll see the same number of responses, but from a larger base, which reduces your success ratio.

- **Make it company wide:** If a subscriber no longer wishes to receive email from your company, make sure the unsubscribe email address is removed from every list in every department throughout your company (if your company has multiple email lists). This is not only good policy, it's the law. The federal CAN-SPAM legislation requires that senders maintain a company-wide "Do-Not-Email" list. If someone wants off, take them off immediately. However, keep reading to learn how to offer options so that folks who just want off one of your lists can be enticed to remain on other lists.

- **Use multiple, convenient unsubscribe methods:** In addition to a link to an unsubscribe page, allow subscribers to unsubscribe by email. This is especially important for those who receive your email newsletter on handhelds or read it offline, for example, on an airplane. These folks can't immediately go to a web page, but they can create an unsubscribe email request to be sent when they sync up or get online again. And don't forget the obvious telephone or snail mail methods. When using these methods, be sure that the receptionist and the mailroom know what to do with these requests. Not only are these practices necessary to ensure that your unsubscribe process is as convenient and thorough as possible, but you'll need them to be compliant with the federal CAN-SPAM legislation.

- **Show a confirmation page:** It's important to confirm a reader's removal from the list as requested. You can do this most efficiently by creating a goodbye page. In addition to putting the requester at ease, you can use this page in a positive manner, by letting users know that the request has been received, that you're sorry to see them go and that perhaps they'll find one of your other newsletters more useful. Perhaps you can entice them to stay with another option, such as receiving the same newsletter less frequently, which may be able to re-capture some recipients. Also, remind them that they are welcome to come back at any time. A brief survey asking why recipients are unsubscribing is also useful in gaining insights into the effectiveness of your newsletter. We talk more about how to use the unsubscribe request as an opportunity to build your list later in this chapter.

- **Send an email confirmation:** There are two schools of thought on this practice. While some believe if someone asks not to get email you shouldn't send another email, others feel that an email confirmation provides greater satisfaction. Consider your audience and the level of trust they have in you. If you do send a confirmation, we recommend that it be sent immediately and be very straightforward content-wise. Of course, unsubscribe requests that are received by email should be confirmed by email. That email might contain the same information as the goodbye page.

- **Include a privacy policy link and fall-back instructions:** As on the subscribe page, it is important to have a link to your privacy policy on the unsubscribe page. Also include an email address and a phone number where you can be contacted if there is a problem, question or comment. Better to have someone call you directly than to be reported as a spammer.

- **Back up the addresses of unsubscribers:** Because one mistake can destroy a relationship forever, make sure your unsubscribe system has a backup data flow. Send a duplicate copy of each unsubscribe to a separate email box or database where it can be retrieved if the main system goes down. If you use an email service provider to send your mail, be sure you know all about their backup procedures, and consider asking them to send a real-time feed to your servers as an additional safeguard. In addition, CAN-SPAM requires that you maintain a list of addresses that have been unsubscribed, as well as those who have subscribed.

Smart Tactics Designed to Reduce Unsubscribe Rates

While it is vital that you take subscribers off the list the instant they request it, there are strategies you can employ to reduce the chances that they will want to go off the list, as well as ones to encourage them to stay on. Many of these have been mentioned earlier, but they bear repeating.

Send good stuff

If your email is fun, interesting and valuable, your unsubscribe rate should be low. Follow the advice in the previous chapters. Figure out what your audience wants to receive and send it to them. If you are seeing jumps in unsubscribe rates, survey your subscribers to find out where your content is lacking.

Offer alternative frequencies

Give consumers the option to change the delivery frequency on the unsubscribe page. What was overwhelming as a daily might feel reasonable as a weekly. The more flexibility you offer, the greater your chance of keeping subscribers.

Offer change of address

This is one of the most common oversights that email marketers make. They offer ways to get on the list and ways to get off the list, but no way to stay on the list with a different address. People change email addresses fairly often, and if it is not immediately obvious to them how they can alert you to the change, they will either unsubscribe altogether or re-subscribe with a new account, leaving you with bad data. In a study conducted by Return Path and the Association for Interactive Marketing, 20% of marketers reported that they do not allow people to update their email addresses.

Offer other newsletters

This is one of the best ways to keep subscribers. By offering multiple newsletters, you give the reader a chance to change topics if they so desire. They can decide to receive your promotional announcements, or a weekly "tip" sheet, or one or several newsletters on specific topics of interest to them. Subscriber interests may change over time. But the important thing is to get them to stay engaged with you via one of your lists. The more options you offer, the more chances you have to keep the conversation going, and that's the best way to maintain a long-term relationship with readers. Remember, the most important part of your commitment to subscribers is your promise to send relevant information. Sometimes, the more targeted the information is to a particular subject, the more relevant it becomes. You may find that one newsletter covering three topics results in fewer overall signups than three newsletters on one specific topic each.

Ask for feedback, and act on it

Customer feedback can offer valuable insight into what's not working about your emails. Every email should offer a feedback link or form. Get input before readers are so annoyed or bored that they want to unsubscribe! The feedback you get will give you ideas for new newsletters and other stories to include, and it will help you make improvements to your program.

In fact, consider having a feedback form on your unsubscribe page. If it is short and easy to complete, you might be surprised at how many people do fill it out. You can also offer a checkbox for permission to re-contact them if you make changes based on their feedback. While few will check this box (and you don't have an inch to play around here—never re-email unsubscribers without explicit permission), those who do comprise a valuable list of people willing to hear from you under certain conditions. We'll cover more about using surveys to get feedback in Chapter 6.

A Stagnant List Is a Depreciating Asset

Many companies have email lists they have never sent email to, because they started collecting addresses long before they decided what they wanted to send. Then there are the lists that haven't been used in a long time because of changes in a company's strategy or budget. For whatever reason, the company ends up sitting on a list of names that hasn't seen an email in quite a while, if at all. This is a terrible waste of valuable customer permission and data, not to mention acquisition effort and hard costs.

Depending on exactly how long it has been dormant, what permission exists and what was sent before, the list may be worthless. Email lists don't have the same shelf life as postal lists. While most people tend to stay in the same home for many years, emails change often and therefore go bad, though you can retain some relationships using list hygiene and Email Change of Address (ECOA) services. Best practices for permission as well as deliverability demand that you implement a testing strategy (which we'll cover in the next section) after three to six months of address inactivity.

Determining the value of an old list

To determine the value of the list, try mailing a reintroduction to spark a memory. Make it very clear to recipients why they are getting the email, and be sure there is an incentive to stay on the list or to provide updated information. This way, you will be able to determine how much of your list is still good, and you might even obtain some valuable additional information. Another useful technique is to mail to the list in segments, all the while monitoring feedback, deliverability and complaints. We suggest mailing to no more than 10% of the entire list at a time—less if you have a very big list or if it has been more than ninety days since the last mailing.

If the list is no longer responsive or clean, well, you've just learned a very important lesson the hard way—keep your list current, clean and well maintained. The reality is that you will need to start building your list once again.

How to Keep Your Email List Clean

As we just discussed, people change their email addresses faster than ever these days. They are switching jobs, changing ISPs and abandoning email boxes that are full of spam. In fact, many industry experts believe that 31% of consumers change their email addresses every year. Jupiter Research predicts that number will be as high as 40% with the increasing availability of broadband in more and more geographic areas.

Sending email to bad addresses wastes money and can cause all of your email to be blocked by ISPs, so you want to make sure that you find and repair or remove bad addresses from your file in a timely manner. By implementing some thoughtful practices, you can minimize this risk.

Have a "change my email address" form on your newsletter or web site

For reasons we just outlined, this is critical. What's more, it is so simple to do, yet so many companies don't bother. Without it, readers who wish to continue receiving your email newsletter are going to need to sign up for your list a second time with their new address, and you'll be left with duplicate addresses and never know which are good and which are bad.

Use an "email change of address" service

Marketers from the direct-mail world are already familiar with a process known as NCOA—National Change of Address. This service allows companies to update their postal files with new addresses for the millions of Americans who move every year. The online equivalent is called Email Change of Address, or ECOA.

Because email is fundamentally different than direct mail, ECOA works differently than NCOA. The process is simple: you give your file to the ECOA company, they compare it to their file and alert you to any available new email addresses as a percent of your list. The next step represents the key difference between NCOA and ECOA: with NCOA, no one ever bothers to ask the consumer if they wish to continue receiving mail from your company. A reputable ECOA company, however, will only give you a new address if the consumer agrees. Remember, a lot of consumers change email addresses to get away from the junk! Don't risk your relationships by sending email to new addresses without the corresponding new permission.

Use a good list server or email service provider (ESP)

If you use a list server—an automated mailing list distribution system—make sure that it isn't mislabeling temporary bad addresses as permanently bad addresses, in other words, confusing "hard" and "soft" bounces. For example, an out-of-office message may report as undeliverable, but the address may actually be good. This is considered a soft bounce. A hard bounce occurs when an "unknown user/mailbox not found" message is reported by the recipient's ISP, indicating that the user's account is no longer active. You will find much more on hard and soft bounces, and how to handle each, later in this chapter. Most good ESPs pride themselves on being able to help with this sort of mapping. In addition, there are third-party and open-source software solutions that can handle these tasks.

Make sure the data comes in correctly

Like all databases, email lists follow the "garbage in, garbage out" rule. There are a number of low-tech and high-tech solutions to help keep your database clean right from the start. First, ask subscribers to enter their email address twice. This can significantly cut down on the number of bad addresses. (Caution, it may also cut down on the total number of addresses, as any extra registration step decreases conversion. Test it!)

Your tech team can also set up scripts to check email addresses for basic hygiene as they come in. This includes testing for known bad or expired domains (e.g., the once-popular ISP @Home is now defunct), common spam trap addresses (as mentioned in Chapter 4, spam traps are fake email addresses created by programmers to identify spammers who use illegal harvesting methods to collect addresses) and common errors (i.e., commas instead of periods, ALO instead of AOL, etc.). Catch these mistakes during the sign-up process and you can immediately alert the subscriber before processing a bad address.

Be on the lookout for malicious activity

Set up a back-end filter that monitors for large numbers of addresses coming from a single IP address. Unless there is a business explanation for this, it could be malicious. For example, a hacker with a grudge might be looking to portray your company as a spammer and add a large number of addresses from unsuspecting subscribers to your list, thus aggravating all those to whom you would then send email. If you see such activity, do not mail to these addresses. Instead, try to isolate them and keep them off your list. There are also third-party software solutions available for this type of monitoring.

The importance of using a good email list hygiene system

In addition to on-going maintenance, as described above, it is always worth your while to use an email list hygiene service that will serve as a silent sentinel, regularly screening for problems that muddy your list. Here's how it works: you send your list to a hygiene vendor, they clean it up and send it back. If you have new data coming in regularly (and you should!) then you should have the new portions of your list checked regularly—at least quarterly, better monthly. Remember, the cleaner your list, the better.

A good service will be on the lookout for the following:

- **Format and syntax errors**: Many email addresses fail to deliver because of format errors generally attributable to data entry or typographical mistakes. For example: Ann.Smith.yahoo.com (no "@" symbol) or Ann.Smith@@yahoo.com (too many "@" symbols).
- **Invalid domains**: The domain is the part of the email address that appears after the "@" sign. Your database should be checked regularly against a list of valid domains, in what is called a Validated Email List Hygiene check. For example, @attbi.com is now @comcast.net. Although Comcast has been forwarding email sent to old attbi.com addresses to their new comcast.net domain since the acquisition, it has announced that it will no longer do so after December 31, 2004. It is dangerous to assume that Jenn187@attbi.com is always going to be Jenn187@comcast.net, since

that may have been a pre-existing address at Comcast. Therefore, always use caution and make sure you understand the ownership and domain-change rules. Never make blanket changes to accommodate domain name changes. On the other hand, if someone enters Jane@xyz.com, there is no way to know what was intended—or if the address was entered incorrectly on purpose. As we mentioned several times, this is a problem that a welcome message, sent immediately upon sign-up, will help to rectify.

- **Common domain typos:** Along with checking the validity of domains, you should be on the lookout for typos that can be corrected. For example, @alo.com is a common typo for @aol.com. You need to use caution, however, since it is not necessarily a given that alo.com is a typo and that this it is not, in fact, a valid domain. So, when constructing rules to clean and update your list, you need to make sure to stay current with the ever-changing domain landscape.

- **Bogus and known bad email addresses:** Every file has its share of intentionally incorrect email addresses. For example, BillGates@microsoft.com or test@test.com. You should establish bogus email address filters, outsource this function or manually check new sign-ups regularly to identify these addresses and flag them for suppression from your email list.

- **Role accounts:** These are addresses for general business email accounts, such as sales@, postmaster@, or info@. These are not ideal; first, role accounts can be spam traps and, second, these accounts are often not being monitored by individuals who will take action on your newsletters.

Dealing Effectively with Human Oversight

No matter how clear and easy you make the unsubscribe process, people will always complain that they were unable to unsubscribe. Some get it wrong; others simply can't follow directions. It's best to anticipate such troubles and understand how to handle them.

Unfortunately, the most thorough way to overcome human oversight is to undertake the tedious task of checking your newsletters' reply address every day and manually processing all unsubscribe requests that were submitted incorrectly to this address. By manually reviewing all replies, you'll identify those who either didn't see or chose to ignore the line that says "Please don't reply to this email."

Finally, the best way to reduce incoming mail volume for the routine matters that are so often the basis for human oversight problems is to clearly spell out your procedures for giving feedback, unsubscribing, placing an order and so forth. Make it clear and easy for people to respond properly and more often than not they will do so.

Lessons from the Inbox: Email Customer Service

The incredible speed of email has spoiled people, particularly when it comes to customer-service issues. Nowadays, when people hit reply or send emails to any address they can find at your company—usually role accounts like info@ or help@, but also subscribe and unsubscribe addresses—they expect a prompt reply. That's easy enough to do if subscribers send emails only to the inboxes that you designate for these purposes, but of course, that doesn't always happen, and it's not that simple. In fact, you'll be amazed at how many questions, comments, orders and more you will receive in virtually every inbox associated with your company. And all of these should be responded to in a timely manner. Ignoring these emails is akin to not picking up the phone when a customer calls you. It's important, so do it.

Have a real, live person monitor all incoming email

Once a day, you or another responsible member of your team should scan every mailbox that consumers could possibly reply to or email, even if you have instructed them not to reply to or contact such mailboxes. This is a crucial exercise, because complaints regarding email are a prime cause of blocking and filtering by ISPs. If these mailboxes cannot be checked every day, you might arrange for an automated reply that is immediately sent that informs the person their email has been received and a representative will respond to their concern within a given amount of time, say twenty-four or forty-eight hours. Then be sure to deliver on that promise. If the reply is a complaint, and the complainer doesn't get a resolution in a timely manner, they might take the complaints to the ISP, and this could cause delivery problems for your entire program.

Don't tell your customers not to reply to the messages you send

First, it's not very customer-friendly. Second, in spite of your request, it is certain that some people will do so anyway, and these emails should be read and addressed in a timely manner. Certain demographics are more likely to misunderstand that emails are often sent by list servers rather than real people. Older and younger customers tend to fall into this group. But all of us are guilty of not reading the fine print. If your customers want to reach you—let them!

Moreover, it is very easy to set up a reply-to link that is different from the "From" address. That way, even if someone hits reply, it will go to where you want so that it can be answered in a timely manner.

Ask for feedback

Since you're responding to customers who obviously have an opinion and want to be heard, this is a fantastic chance to find out what's not working with your emails, so always be sure to ask for feedback through a link to a simple form. If feedback is consistent, use it to make improvements to your program.

Handle spam complaints the right way

First, apologize. People get upset for all sorts of reasons, and email provides a great forum to rant. Often, a sincerely written apology will defuse a potentially volatile situation.

You can also prove you didn't spam. Some people forget or get confused, so you may need to provide the complainer with the time, date and IP address to remind them that they signed up. Your list host or IT department can give you this information. This is critical information to have, because if an issue is ever raised by an ISP, you can produce proof that your emails have indeed been requested and that you are not a spammer.

Finally, make sure to get the complainer off your list. If someone doesn't want your email, don't send email to them. A real human (not an automated server) should double-check that the recipient has been unsubscribed correctly. In addition to folks who have unsubscribed and gone away quietly, there are complainers and activists who will sign up again to get more email in the hopes of embarrassing you. If you suspect that, put the complainer on your "do-not-email" list, and check it regularly against new subscribers.

Educate the Entire Company about Email Policies and Procedures

The entire staff must be clear that the task of sending email to your customer or subscriber base is one your company takes seriously. Make sure everyone is aware of all of your policies. It's incredibly easy for an eager junior marketer or sales person to blast a campaign to thousands of customers from his or her desk, or from the mass-email software now built into most contact-management databases. Unless this type of action is prohibited or properly monitored and regulated, it will surely happen. Your policies regarding email blasting should be part of new employee training and orientation programs as well as the subject of a company-wide quarterly email message.

The Importance of Creating Backups of Your Lists

We recommend you back up your subscriber lists on a regular basis—at least weekly. Considering the value of these lists, you don't want to have a single copy sitting in isolation anywhere. Archive all subscribe requests, including the time and IP address of each subscriber, since this is your only way to prove that someone signed up for your list. This is valuable information to have on hand if these folks accuse you of spamming them, which, incidentally, happens frequently. And backing up this data is not only critical, it is mandatory to remain legally compliant, as CAN-SPAM requires that you maintain a list of consumers who have unsubscribed as well as those who have subscribed.

Quarantine New Data

If you are acquiring addresses through list acquisition deals, particularly co-registration programs, we recommend mailing to these addresses from a separate IP address, at least for the first several mailings. In doing so, you can assess the quality of the data partner by measuring complaint and unknown user rates. You must determine your own threshold for acceptable complaint levels, but anything approaching 1% is generally considered problematic and could lead to blocking.

Bounce Processing: What It Is and Why It Matters

As we mentioned earlier, bounces are important to your email program because they indicate potential delivery problems and because properly managing them is an effective way to keep your list clean. If improperly managed, however, bounces can lead you to remove people from your list unnecessarily. How you handle bounces is a strategic consideration for keeping your list up to date and maintaining consistent deliverability to ISPs.

There are four general categories of bounces you'll encounter:

- **"Unknown User" hard bounces**: These indicate a malformed or non-existent email address. The email address may be inaccurate either because the user entered the wrong address (on purpose or not) or because the recipient has changed email addresses. Regardless of the reason, "Unknown Users" should be removed from your list, because they are not deliverable and a high unknown user rate will make you look like a spammer. However, it is possible to get an incorrect unknown user bounce because of a problem at the ISP. We recommend setting your server to make two tries within a certain period of time (which will depend on how often you send email) then pull that address off your list. And don't forget to subtract these hard bounces from your total list size when calculating your response rates so your metrics are accurate.

- **"Blocked" hard bounces**: These indicate that your mail is being rejected by the receiving mail server. Addresses associated with a "blocked" hard bounce should not be removed from your list. You should, however, refrain from mailing addresses at these domain(s) until the block has been lifted.

- **Transient bounces**: These are notifications that an email did not yet make it to the inbox, or that the recipient will not receive it for some period of time. For example, you may receive a "delayed delivery" notice because of a slowdown somewhere en route between your server and the recipient's server. "Out of office" notices may also be considered transient, as they may have been received—depending on how the end user has set up their system. In any case, these bounces can generally be ignored unless they happen repeatedly to one address or a particular domain.

- **Soft bounces**: These occur when the receiving mail server is temporarily unable to accept your mail. There are a variety of reasons you might receive a soft bounce, ranging from the mailbox being full to the receiving server being too busy to accept mail when you are transmitting. Because there is a high probability that you will be able to deliver these messages at a later date, you can be more liberal when deciding whether or not to keep the addresses on your list. Nevertheless, repeatedly and consistently receiving a soft bounce for an address can indicate a bad address. For example, a "mailbox full" return for an extended period of time probably means that the mailbox has been abandoned. Your IT department or email deliverability experts should be able to help you interpret the causes behind your soft bounces so you can make informed decisions regarding address suspensions or deletions. Guidelines for setting bounce management rules can be found in the next section.

The Art of Bounce Management

Not all bounces generate the standard "mailer-daemon" email response we're used to seeing in our inboxes, but nearly all generate a response code in your SMTP log files. These are the files that keep track of every conversation between your email server and receiving servers. Closely monitoring your log files will allow you to take immediate action to solve any problems you discover.

A high bounce rate can have a negative impact on your overall delivery rate. This can, in turn, affect all of your email campaigns, not just the ones triggering bounces. If your IP address is associated with too many "unknown user" bounces at a particular ISP, you risk being blacklisted or blocked by that ISP. Therefore, keeping your list clean of unknown users is a cornerstone to your email delivery success.

Whether you send email in-house or through an email service provider, your bounce-management process should reflect how often you email, the size of your list and the nuances of bounce reporting. Specifically:

- **Set "bounce rules."** You need to define how many bounces you will incur before removing an email from your list. The standard rule is that an email should be removed after two "unknown user" hard bounces or three soft bounces over a period greater than fourteen days. An "unknown user" hard bounce indicates that the mailbox no longer exists. A soft bounce could be an "I'm busy, come back later" error. The time period for removal varies, based on how often you send mail. If you mail daily, for example, you can tolerate more bounces than if you mail monthly.

- **Define a "bounce" with customers in mind.** Some email platforms can inadvertently categorize a temporary email account status, such as "out of office" replies, as a hard bounce. This can lead to unnecessary removal of email addresses from your list. Just because someone doesn't want to read your email while they are vacationing on the beach, it doesn't mean they won't want it once they return. One solution to this phenomenon is to allow subscribers to put mailings "on hold" through an option in a preference center, just as they might stop having their newspaper delivered while out of town.

- **Manage bounces by ISP.** While your overall bounce percentages are good to know and understand, problems will be uncovered faster if you look at your bounces by ISP. A bounce rate of 4% or 5% across your whole list is not too troubling. However, if the majority of those bounces all come back from one ISP—and if they represent the majority, or even the totality, of the email addresses you have for that ISP—this indicates a problem beyond normal email churn. While free accounts (such as Yahoo! and Hotmail) will have a higher churn rate than paid accounts (like AOL and Earthlink), your bounces should be fairly even across ISPs and should stay consistent from campaign to campaign. By breaking this information down by ISP, for every campaign, you will pick up on deliverability problems much more quickly.
- **Look beyond the obvious.** The bounces you see are one thing, but the information you don't see can be of even more interest. There is a wealth of information about each bounce response in your SMTP log files. These files record every conversation between your server and the receiving email servers (e.g., ISPs). When your email is blocked, the log files often reveal why. Analyzing these files can point to problems you are having at particular mail servers. For this reason, make sure that you, your IT team and your email deliverability experts are reviewing them on a regular basis.
- **Remember that blocks and bounces are not the same.** If you remove an address from your file because of a general ISP blocking message, you will be removing a potentially good customer. Make sure you separate true bounces, where the email address is no longer valid, from messages that indicate that a valid address is being blocked by the server, and treat them differently. When you resolve a block, re-mail to your subscribers at that domain to confirm that delivery has resumed.

As we mentioned at the beginning of this chapter, your list is a valuable asset and should be treated as such. Keep it clean. Maintain it. Protect it. Put the systems in place now to keep your company in good standing with your subscribers and prospects.

Part II: List Strategies Summary

- Never send an email without the permission of the recipient. Otherwise, you risk alienating customers, being labeled a spammer and having all your email messages blocked by ISPs and corporate system administrators.

- There are five levels of permission. Opt-out, where a person must choose not to receive future mailings from you. Negative opt-in, where you offer consumers an email subscribe form, usually as part of an order form of some other kind, and place a pre-checked box for an agreement to receive emails that a person must uncheck in order not to receive the newsletter. Opt-in requires a subscriber to proactively check a box in order to receive your newsletter. Confirmed opt-in sends an email message to new subscribers confirming their subscription and offering them the option to unsubscribe immediately if the subscription was in any way a mistake. Double opt-in (sometimes referred to as verified opt-in) sends an email message to new subscribers confirming their subscription and requiring them to respond to the email in order to begin the subscription.

- There are two general methods to build an email list: Organic, which enables you to create your own list using free techniques, and Paid Acquisition, which consists of list rental, partnerships and advertising.

- Once you have your list in place, put systems in place to maintain it to preserve its value and relevance.

- Unsubscribe requests are a natural occurrence. Expect them and know how to handle them properly in order to maintain a positive image in the hopes of future dealings with unsubscribers. Make it easy to unsubscribe to your newsletter.

- To reduce unsubscribes, try offering options such as different newsletters or reduced frequency of delivery.

- Make sure your list stays clean and current by providing change-of-address forms, using a good list server, making sure all data is received correctly, using a good email list hygiene system, using email change-of-address companies, properly processing all of your bounces and watching out for malicious activity.

- A stagnant list is a depreciating asset. Because people change email addresses often, if you don't send email regularly, or at all, your list may very well be worthless.

PART III

Optimization Strategies

If the measure of a good newsletter is relevance, the measure of a successful email newsletter program is return on investment (ROI). Prove your ROI and you can rest assured that your company's higher-ups will start to share your enthusiasm for email marketing.

The final four chapters will teach you how to measure, determine and, most importantly, optimize the effectiveness of your email newsletter campaign.

Chapter 6: The Importance of Testing (and Re-testing)

The biggest a-ha! moment came for us when we realized the long-term value of testing some aspect of every email we send. Not only do the small improvements add up, but we are able to carry learning forward from one campaign to the next, so we are constantly improving the whole program.

—Beth Fisher, web marketing strategist,
American Management Association

All forms of direct marketing are, by nature, testing intensive. Every aspect of an effort—from the headline to the teasers to the offer to the packaging—should be tested and retested to ensure maximum impact. Email allows you to take that testing to new heights.

Because it is uniquely interactive and fast, email is arguably the most powerful medium available for fast, thorough testing. In fact, the immediacy and interactivity of email can provide almost instantaneous feedback from recipients. There is no reason not to test before almost every mailing. Even a small, simple test of subject lines can drive major changes in response.

Setting Up a Testing Program

Not every part of every message needs to be—or should be—tested with every mailing. Be strategic by testing specific components periodically. We recommend starting with those tried and true items that have consistently been among those tested most often in direct marketing for years, more specifically the teaser, the headline and the offer, since these are often the three most powerful elements in motivating a reader to take action. We'll help you think a little more broadly about that in this chapter.

We also recommend you construct small tests right away, even before you make any changes to your program based on the advice in this book. This will start to give you some information with which to benchmark your program. (If you're not sure where to start, we'll provide you with some pointers later in this chapter.)

A word of warning: Don't use your entire customer base as a test market, because the sheer volume may make it impossible for you to determine which variables are working better than others with any accuracy. Instead, set up test lists of addresses that are reserved for experimenting. This limits your risk and still enables you to test extensively. Depending on the size of your list, testing should be done on no more than 10% of the list. So, if you have a list of 30,000 names, select three sets of 1,000 recipients from your list. Send your message with a different subject line to each list. By monitoring the open rates, you'll know within a few hours which subject line is getting the best response. Then, using that subject line, send the mailing to the remaining 27,000 subscribers.

Think about it: In about an hour you can greatly improve the success rate of your campaigns at no additional expense. This example is so simple and effective, there's no reason not to do this every time.

Considering all of the elements that go into an email newsletter, you have an unlimited number of variables that you can test. But here are some of the more important ones on which to focus your attention:

Subject lines

As we mentioned earlier, this is a quick, easy and powerful way to increase the effectiveness of your email. From a traditional advertising or direct-mail perspective, it is like being able to test multiple headlines or envelope teaser lines, only it is dynamic, so you can test it directly with your subscriber base and make well-informed decisions mere moments before launch. Now that's testing power!

Consider This: Subject Line Testing Idea!

You can also use search engines to test subject lines. This method does come with a cost, albeit a low one since most search engines let you buy cheap pay-per-click listings. Here's how: Create five to ten subject lines for the same offer and list them all simultaneously on a search engine, using the same search term. Then simply track which one gets the most clicks. Usually, the phrase that wins in a search will be the most effective in an email.

Offer sequence and placement

Try putting different offers in different places throughout the newsletter. This will help you determine where to place your most important items. Some spots—like the upper right-hand corner—tend to get more clicks, but you'll only find out what works best for your design by rotating your offers. This is an old trick of web site editors: place links to the same article or feature in several spots with varied headlines and see what works best, then optimize around it. You can use this same strategy for email. Try some at the top, some at the bottom and some on the side, and see which spots pull best. Then reserve those spaces for your most important offers. We've found that the placement sometimes matters more than the offer.

Number of offers

Direct-marketing norms stipulate one mail, one offer. That holds true in email, and current trends show response rates increasing with fewer offers per email. This is most likely due to the basic fact that clutter is confusing. But consumer response regarding the best ratio of offers to email changes rapidly, so test new combinations of content, offers and offer quantity on a frequent basis.

Always consider your audience and your level of trust, as well. Parenting sites, for example, can usually have lots of various content and offers, because moms have a variety of needs related to taking care of children. On the other hand, business-to-business marketers usually need to stay focused on one topic to hold the attention of busy executives in their target market. To test this trend correctly, keep your templates consistent. This will allow you to compare apples to apples. Then you can start modifying the offers and their placement.

Mailing frequency

As we discussed in Chapter 2, the frequency of your mailings is important. How often you mail is often determined by your content. For example, if you're sending out top headlines, you'll want to mail daily. If you're providing "Things to Do on the Weekend," weekly is the obvious frequency. But since most content isn't so clear cut, you don't want to guess on this aspect. For starters, always ask subscribers their preferred frequency when they sign up.

Timing of your mailings

Believe it or not, even the time of day can have a major impact on results. Depending on what you're marketing and the type of content you're distributing, it may be more to your advantage to mail first thing in the morning, or near the close of business. For example, many e-tailers find that they get great bumps in sales if they mail right before lunch, because lots of folks spend their lunchtime running personal online errands, such as buying gifts, ordering books, planning trips, etc.

This maybe due in part to deliverability issues. Return Path recently did a study and found that delivery rates across the top ISPs vary with time and day that mail is sent. For example, there was a drop in deliverability from 9 A.M. to 3 P.M. Eastern Time—a time when SpamCop finds the highest incidence of spam reporting. Find a balance between optimum response and deliverability for your audience.

Here's an easy way to find out what will work best for you: Divide your list into ten parts and send the same message at ten different times throughout the week, tracking which gets the best response. It's easy to do, and even a 1% jump in response can make a serious dent in the bottom line. Repeat this test every three or four months.

Content length and order

The ideal length and number of stories for your email newsletter program varies depending on what your audience prefers. Try one story about one paragraph in length, by itself, and then try the same story with several promotional add-ons. Then review your readers' response by measuring click rates and pass-along rates. Ask for feedback, as well.

And don't forget about wording. Some words and phrases just pull better than others, whether as part of subject lines or in email headlines. For example, the editor of a prominent content and community site once tested the headlines "Celebrate the Holidays" and "Celebrate Christmas." Both linked to the same exact page, but the second one got a far higher number of clicks. You can do tests like this in your emails and on your web site to determine what words hit your audience's hot buttons.

Landing Pages

Always use a custom landing page that highlights the specific offer and streamlines the call to action. Never dump folks onto your homepage and expect them to navigate to the information or offer promised in your email by themselves. Think about when you call an 800 number to purchase a product. The operator who answers the phone doesn't simply say, "Hello." They are prepared with scripted greetings that guide the caller through the purchase process. For every offer, test multiple versions of the landing page, each with variations in copy and design. Even a 5% jump in the close rate will make a big difference in your bottom line. A slightly better landing page can change the story of your entire email campaign.

Amazon.com does a great job connecting their email promotions and landing pages, both from a writing and a design perspective. The email (top) carries the more recognizable elements of the Amazon.com site, including the logo, "Your Personal Picks" recommendation, and the ever-recognizable "Add to Cart" icon.

Once someone clicks on either the book, book title or "Add to Cart" icon, they are taken to the landing page (bottom), where they are greeted by the familiar Amazon.com bookstore page. This smart execution creates an almost seamless transition that makes the purchase process fast and easy.

Newsletter designs

As we mentioned in the Chapter 3, a design that is unattractive, cluttered, clunky or in other ways difficult to read will work against you. Try sending the same content plugged into several different templates to three groups of test subscribers, along with a survey asking their opinions on the design. Then review the survey results with the response rates of each template to determine which design is most effective.

The moral of the story? Test, test, test. Test every aspect of your email campaign—particularly those outlined above—on an ongoing basis. Considering the speed with which you can obtain and act upon the feedback, there's simply no reason not to.

Use Surveys to Obtain User Feedback

We've mentioned it several times in previous chapters, but it bears repeating: Continually request feedback from your subscribers by using short, interactive surveys. This is the best way to learn whether or not your newsletter is relevant. You'll also determine what does and doesn't work with your email newsletter and what changes your readers would like to see.

Ask them. They'll tell you. And they'll be honest. Remember, these customers have requested to receive email from you, so they have a vested interest in making sure that the time they spend reading your newsletter is indeed time well spent.

As with most online activities, shorter is better when it comes to surveys. The direct-mail golden rule is "no more than seven questions." Start from there and then try surveys of varying length to determine the ideal number of questions for your audience. And remember, people are always more interested in anything that clearly benefits them. The more you can focus the questions on their needs and interests, the better the response will be—and the better the feedback.

The easiest way to do a survey by email is to send a text message with a link to the survey form online. You can present this either as a standalone mailing or as a link in your regular newsletter. Your level of permission for email and relationship with your subscribers will dictate the best approach. If you hope to do surveys often, consider asking subscribers to sign up specifically for a Customer Opinion Board or something like that. Remember the cardinal rule of self-segmentation: customers who raise their hand and offer to tell you what they think are going to yield higher responses.

You can also embed survey forms right into HTML email messages. Again, you can do this as a one-off mailing or within your newsletter. There is evidence that embedded forms yield higher response rates, but they can sometimes cause problems in certain email programs, so test carefully. However, if it does work for your audience and your software can handle it, consider putting a question or two in every newsletter. Over time you will be able to amass a warehouse of information about your subscribers.

MOVING AHEAD One-Year Anniversary Survey — Edit this survey
1. MOVING AHEAD Survey

Welcome to the MOVING AHEAD survey. A hearty "Thank you" for your willingness to participate! We've tried to keep it as simple and painless as possible. Every answer is important, so dig in!

1. I read MOVING AHEAD:
- Every time it comes
- Some of the time
- Never

2. I like to receive MOVING AHEAD in:
- HTML format
- Text format
- No preference

3. The best time of day for me to read MOVING AHEAD is:
- In the morning (8-11 am)
- At lunchtime (11 am-2 pm)
- In the afternoon (2-5 pm)
- After work (after 5 pm)

6. The parts of MOVING AHEAD I enjoy most are:

	Really enjoy	Enjoy	Neutral	Dislike	Really dislike
"How to" or "Ten tips"-type articles					
Interviews with authors or experts					
Free book chapters					
Self-assessments/self-tests					
Special offers and announcements					

10. The maximum amount of times I would like to receive e-mail from AMA (including MOVING AHEAD) is:
- Whenever AMA has information or promotional offers for me
- Every week
- Every two weeks
- Once a month
- Once a quarter

© Copyright 2004 American Management Association. All Rights Reserved.
Reprinted with permission.

When the American Management Association wanted to find out how their newsletter was being perceived by readers, they sent a text email with a link to this survey, hosted on SurveyMonkey. As you can see, they gathered a lot of great information on subscribers' feelings about timing, frequency, content, format and more. Now *that's* a great customer-feedback form!

Chapter 7: Measuring Success One Number at a Time

At the end of the day, it all comes down to numbers. Great content and good design don't mean much if you can't get readers to open the email and take action. A huge audience is only as good as its ability to drive revenue—whether in the form of advertising dollars or sales (or, as is increasingly common, both!). We believe that watching our numbers closely is crucial to the overall success of our program—and by extension our business.

—Chris Michel, president, Military Advantage

Marketers are funny creatures. At one end of the spectrum, there are marketers who within minutes of hitting "send" on an email campaign will run into the IT department or call their ESP and ask frantically, "Well, how'd it do?" demanding the most particular details about the performance. And at the other end, there are marketers who haven't the faintest idea of whether or not their email marketing efforts are effective. They don't even know what questions to ask to make that determination. They're comfortable with the old mass-marketing adage: "I know that half of my marketing is effective; I'm just not sure which half."

The ideal is to be somewhere in the middle: Plan ahead so you know which metrics to track, then work with your IT and operations teams to retrieve the data in a timely manner, and evaluate results based on relative performance as well as industry benchmarks. Don't worry. It's not hard. We'll identify some of the most important email metrics and tell you what they mean.

The Key Point When Analyzing Metrics

Before we get into the specific metrics, an important point needs to be made. You must always compare apples to apples. It is crucial that you look at the same numbers in the same way across campaigns. Be on the lookout for any jumps or dips in clicks, opens, subscribes and unsubscribes. If you get steady or growing response rates, you know that you have a good list and are sending relevant content and a proper balance of effective marketing messages. A drop in response rates indicates list fatigue, over-mailing and saturation. If your metrics imply that your mailing program is amiss, ask for feedback by surveying your subscribers regarding the issues. They'll tell you the truth. Then you can make the important and necessary changes. Don't be afraid to break some china to improve your ROI.

Key Metrics for Tracking Results

These are the basic metrics that define the success of your email campaign. The better you know them and feel comfortable discussing them, the easier it will be for you to understand where your program is succeeding and where it needs help. Bottom line: you need to understand these metrics in order to make the ongoing adjustments and improvements necessary to sustain a long-term, effective email newsletter program.

All about opens

The first metric that most email marketers look at is "opens," which is the number of times your email messages are viewed by users. There are two kinds of opens: Unique opens and total opens. Here's the difference:

- **Total opens:** the number of times your messages are opened. This isn't the best indicator of success, because your number of total opens reflects multiple opens by a single recipient. Therefore, if a subscriber opens your email, skims it quickly, closes it and opens it again later to read it in more depth, you'll see two opens, even though it's the same subscriber. In particular, preview panes—as you find in Outlook—can contribute to high total opens. If a user stops on the preview pane long enough for the graphics to display, the server will count this as an open.
- **Unique opens:** the number of individual recipients who open your message. This is usually the true measure of success, because you know exactly how many of your subscribers are interested enough to open your email.

The open rate is the primary indicator of a successful email newsletter program and a great way to measure whether your content remains relevant. If your open rate is steadily declining, perhaps you're losing touch with your subscribers. It's time to re-think your content and start opening the lines of communication for feedback.

Of course, open rates can tell you a lot about your subject lines. It's helpful to look at opens both from campaign to campaign and then across the course of the campaign. Blips up and down from one newsletter to the next can generally be ascribed to hits or misses with subject lines. A steady increase or decrease over time—absent a comparable increase or decrease in list size—indicates a deeper connection, or lack thereof, with your audience.

Open rates are also helpful in determining the optimum timing of your emails. Watch the days and times related to your opens. Most of your opens will happen within a very tight window around the time the mailing is sent. If there's a significant yet consistent delay in your open rate, you might want to consider sending your mailing closer to the time when your subscribers are opening your email. In addition, you can even detect patterns in forwarding by looking to see if a significant number of emails get opened days, or even weeks, later.

One final—and key—point: open rate can only be measured on HTML campaigns, since it requires the use of a tracking meta tag (usually embedded in an invisible graphic) to alert the server that the email has been opened.

Clicks and click-throughs

While clicks, the total number of times that a given link is clicked on, is an indicator of response to your emails, a more accurate measure is the "click-through rate" (CTR), which expresses the number of clicks as a percentage. There are two popular ways to calculate CTR. One is by dividing the number of unique HTML opens by the number of HTML clicks. For example, if your mailing had 1,000 opens and 200 clicks to your site, your CTR was 20%. (Note: This calculation is only possible with HTML emails, since text emails don't record opens.)

The other way to calculate CTR is to divide the number of clicks by the total number of emails sent. The advantage is that you can include text messages in this calculation. The disadvantage is that the percentage will be lower, since you are counting people who didn't open the message—either because it didn't interest them or because they didn't get it. We'll discuss messages that go missing in more detail in Chapter 8.

If you send HTML emails, it definitely makes sense to calculate the CTR based on the open rate, thus tracking how well you did among actual viewers of each email. That said, it's best to track both metrics, especially if you're mailing to a mix of HTML and text users. This is the best was to get an accurate measure of your program's performance.

An additional wrinkle in calculating this metric appears if you use multi-part messaging, as described in Chapter 3. As you'll recall, this technology allows you to send multiple versions of a message (i.e., HTML and text) to the whole list, and the email client on the receiving end will display their highest supported version. Depending on how your system is set up, you may or may not be able to discern how many people see HTML vs. text. Talk with your tech team or your ESP to make sure you understand the reports you get.

The importance of conversion

While it's helpful to monitor opens and clicks, conversion is where the proverbial rubber meets the road, so pay close attention to the percentage of opens, clicks and total list members who take each of your desired actions (buy, forward or subscribe). The true story of the success of your program will be told once you look at all of these numbers in relation to each other.

For example, if your open and click rate is high but your conversion rate is low, this indicates that you are succeeding in getting their attention but that they're simply not buying. The problem then maybe be the product, or perhaps there is a disconnect between what was promised and what is delivered on the landing page. Or, the landing page may be problematic. As you work with these numbers more, patterns will start to emerge, giving you the confidence to test new strategies.

When calculating conversion, always remember not to limit yourself to overnight or same-day results as the way to judge success. While you may get some quick hits, many of your consumers will make their purchasing decisions more slowly than others, particularly if your product or service is a more expensive, or "considered," purchase. Email marketing should be part of a long-term strategy, so examine the numbers over a longer period of time.

Returned emails, or "bounces"

As we discussed in detail in Chapter 5, bounces are messages that don't make it to the inbox. The "bounce rate" is the number of those messages divided by your total list size. There are two types of bounces you'll experience: hard bounces, which are simply bad email addresses, and soft bounces, which are those that are only temporarily not accepting messages, such as "Mailbox full" replies. Simply put, a high bounce rate means you have old or bad data. Bounces must always be an important part of your tracking systems. Your goal is to be a low-bounce sender, because ISPs often look to the number of bounces, in particular hard bounces, to identify potential spammers.

Subscribe and unsubscribe rates

Keep a close eye on your subscribe rate over time. You want to make sure that you understand how the list is growing over the long term, after each mailing and after specific marketing promotions or changes to your web site that are designed to drive new customers and new subscriptions. Sudden jumps may indicate that a particular issue was well received and probably forwarded. You obviously touched a nerve in a good way!

At the same time, watch for sharp jumps in unsubscribes. This may be an indication that something about your mailing has scared away readers and is far less likely to do with anything external to your email program. As a general rule, it is common to see a tiny spike of unsubscribes immediately after a mailing—this is mostly due to newer subscribers who don't remember signing up or longer-term subscribers who've been meaning to unsubscribe and whose memory was sparked by your newsletter.

More Comprehensive Metrics That Reveal In-Depth Information

Once you get comfortable with these basic key metrics, you are ready to go more in depth. After digging deeper into the metrics below you will have a much more thorough sense of the success of your program.

Capture rate

This is the number of people who come to your homepage vs. the size of your list. We recommend you set a goal that no one should leave your site without subscribing to one of your email newsletters. This means that the number of unique visitors and the number of addresses on your list should be relatively close. (While tracking the number of sign-ups to your list is easy, tracking unique visitors is not always so simple. Check with your IT team to make sure you are getting the most accurate numbers possible.)

If these numbers are not close, you need to make sure that email collection is treated as a top priority. For example, if your site averages 50,000 unique visitors per month, yet your list has only 15,000 email addresses, it's time to revisit your email collection strategy. Start to use opt-in forms in all visible, highly trafficked locations, make sure that signing up is easy, provide compelling reasons to sign up and create enticing calls to action. Review Chapter 4 for more tips and strategies on how to turn your web site into an email-capture machine.

And it should be said that this one-to-one ratio is really just a starting point. Depending on the type of site, the make up of your audience and a host of other factors, it may be feasible to have a list that is much bigger than your monthly number of unique visitors. Ultimately, you want identify the universe of people who could be customers for your product or service and aim for that number.

For example, the NPD Consulting Group estimates that there are approximately 2.5 million engaged women in the U.S. and that 71% of them research wedding dresses online. That's over 1.7 million women. If you sell wedding dresses online, that is your known universe of prospects.

Subscription form completion rate

Ideally, you are using a mini-subscribe form throughout your site to maximize your capture of email addresses on every page. However, you may also need to have an actual subscribe page for times when a mini-form isn't possible or appropriate.

If you do have such a page, you'll want to calculate its completion rate—the percentage of people who click on the page and then actually complete the form and submit their information. This should be close to 100%. If it's not, there's something wrong. Sound overly ambitious? It's not. Think about it: Someone clicked on a link to subscribe to your newsletter, landed on the subscribe page but then didn't hit the submit button. What made them change their mind?

The answer is obvious: the subscribe page or process turned them off. If the completion rate on your subscribe forms is low, this is the easiest and fastest metric to improve. If the number on your current form is below 80%, spend some time incorporating some of the tactics mentioned in Chapter 4. Even a few percentage points will add up to huge gains. Keep working on the form until you achieve an average of better than 90% completes.

First issue unsubscribe rate

If you're one of those frustrated marketers who enjoy high sign-up rates only to see a spike in unsubscribe requests following the first issue sent, you're going to need to figure out how to plug this hole to keep your list numbers from sinking. If you have a list that isn't growing and can't figure out why, dig into the metrics and see if you can figure out if subscribers are opting out after the first or second mailing.

Here are the primary causes for a high rate of first issue unsubscribes:

- **Poor content**: If people are signing up, you can rest assured that the topic is exciting to them. But when they drop off just as fast, it could be a sign that something is wrong with your content. Deliver what you promise and promise only what you can deliver. People aren't willing to spend time reading useless emails. Ask yourself some hard questions: Did you promote a newsletter but only send ads? Are you giving in to the requests for more marketing and less information? Is your writer as good as you first thought? Is your design template getting in the way of the message? Ask these hard questions and find the honest answers that will help you get to the bottom of your content problem, fast.

- **No "welcome" message, or a bad one:** Quite often, subscribers will either forget they signed up or not recognize the email is one that they asked for. So remind them, by always sending a welcome message immediately after they sign up and by making sure the format is the same as the newsletter to build familiarity. If you already send a welcome message and you're still getting a high rate of first issue unsubscribes, make sure not only that your welcome message is sincere but that it continues to offer the same enticing content as your sign-up page. It should be short and sweet—all you need to do is welcome them aboard. But do let new subscribers know about the additional content they now have access to as subscribers, including exclusive promotions and invitations. Of course, you can invite new subscribers to take surveys, download coupons or even provide additional information about themselves in return for even more valuable content, say, limited-edition whitepapers.

- **Weak or confusing opt-in:** As we discussed in Chapter 4, a good, strong opt-in will help verify and reinforce a subscriber's interest. If, however, you are vague or, worse yet, sneaky in how you collect the email address, you have not truly gained this person's permission. Remember the first rule of email marketing. If you don't have permission, you've got nothing.

- **Too much time between sign-up and mailing:** It's always a good idea to send an email to new subscribers right away, just to make sure they learn to expect your email. If someone signs up for your quarterly newsletter the day after you just mailed one, it will be four months before they get your next issue. Rather than risk them forgetting, always send new subscribers your latest issue, particularly if your issues are spread out over a period of a month or quarter.

Turn-off rate

Here's something you really want to avoid: angering customers with an email. No matter how professionally you behave, there will inevitably be folks who will be angered by your email and unsubscribe.

Unlike the other metrics in this section, turn-off rate is not easily conveyed in a calculation. It's a theoretical ratio of the total number of emails sent to the number of recipients who took no action (no opens, clicks or sales). Think about it this way: if you send 1,000 messages and convert 20, that's 2%. So, how many of the other 98% have been turned off?

The key to turning off the fewest recipients possible is being careful not to perform the activities that most often raise their ire, such as:

- **Sending email to an appended list.** As discussed in Chapter 4, appending your list is when you have some information on a person and you pay to have a data house supply you with additional information. In this case, let's assume you have 10,000 postal address records and pay to have a third party supply you with the email addresses for these folks. You then mail to them. You certainly did not get their permission to send them email, even though they may be customers (and despite the fact that your action is well within the boundaries prescribed by federal CAN-SPAM legislation). Yet, they are not expecting email from you, and so it is likely you will be viewed as a spammer. You risk alienating good customers, generating complaints and getting blocked by ISPs. Try emailing them once with an acknowledgement of your offline relationship and ask for permission to send additional newsletters. While using email to ask for permission to email is tricky, it can work for some marketers. We'd certainly recommend that this message be opt-in—meaning the recipient would need to take some action to continue receiving email from you.

- **Selling too hard, too fast.** This is a typical mistake by first-time email marketers. They get the addresses and then ram sales messages down the pipeline. While this tactic may generate a sales boost initially, you are sacrificing long-term customer relationships for short-term sales. Remember, in a well-crafted email newsletter program, your audience signs up for relevant, quality content, not just ads.

- **Sending large quantities of email.** Extra mailings may drive more sales, but don't overdo it. A fast increase in sales may cost you dearly in the long run if you burn good relationships with subscribers, who have signed up for a newsletter and are now getting more than they bargained for.

Complaint rates

In their on-going battle to spare customers an inbox full of spam, ISPs in increasing numbers are providing a "This is spam" button. Clicking on this button usually removes the offending email from the inbox and prevents any additional mail from the sender from getting delivered to that inbox. Many ISPs also use these complaints as a factor to identify email to block from everyone's inbox. Therefore, the complaints of a few of your subscribers can prevent you from making it to the inbox of all your subscribers. When you consider that consumers don't realize—or care—that their complaint blocks you from everyone else, or that their definition of spam may be liberal, it quickly becomes clear that you need to know how many people are hitting that button in response to your email.

How do you find that out? Unfortunately, it's not easy. Most of the major ISPs do not provide this information to marketers in any consistent or action-able way. The exception—and it's a big one—is AOL. AOL has set up a free feedback loop service. Fill out the easy-to-use Feedback Loop Request Form (http://postmaster.info.aol.com/tools/fbl.html) and AOL will forward any mail that is reported as spam from subscribers using the AOL "This is spam" button. You must immediately remove these names from your list! This also makes it easy to calculate your AOL complaint rate: just divide the number of complaints received over a set period of time by the number of AOL subscribers who you sent emails to during that same period of time. Other ISPs are considering a feedback loop, but as of press time, none had instituted one. In the absence of this data, AOL benchmarks are your best bet.

The biggest question many marketers ask is "What is an acceptable complaint rate?" None of the ISPs, including AOL, have a published threshold. And the truth is, it depends. Generally, complaint rate is factored against other troubling behavior to separate the good mailers from the bad. (See Chapter 8 for more detail on deliverability.) As a general rule, you want to aim for less than 0.1%. Marketers really start to see problems at the 0.9% mark, but when other factors (such as high unknown users rates) are also a problem, the threshold for com-plaints may be lower.

You should also be measuring the rate of complaints that come directly to you. Again, divide the number of complaints that come through (remember to check all the email boxes where customers might write) by the number of messages that you have sent. Assume that whatever number you arrive at, the number of people who hit "This is spam" is higher and make adjustments accordingly.

Inbox delivery rate

Unfortunately, a percentage of your messages will simply never get delivered to the customers' inboxes due to overly aggressive spam filters. While spam filters are created with good intentions (they are supposed to keep the bad stuff out of cus-tomers' inboxes so the inboxes are clean for personal, business and requested mail), they don't always work properly in the eyes of publishers and marketers. In many cases, overly aggressive filtering is not your friend, as all the efforts you make to build your list and create appealing messages are wasted if the messages aren't making it to the inbox.

One of the most frustrating aspects of blocked and filtered email is that it fre-quently does not bounce back to you; it just gets deleted by the recipient's server or shuttered off to a junk mail folder, never to be seen.

To determine if you have a blocking or filtering problem, look for unexplained drops in your open rate, especially if these instances come from the same ISPs. This is a sign that they may not be getting your email. The best way to calculate your inbox delivery rate accurately is to seed every mailing with a statistically significant number of test names for every major ISP, then see what percentage of the mailings end up in the inbox. In Chapter 8 we'll discuss in more detail how to do this.

A Quick Guide to Calculating Email Metrics

To find out the:	Use this calculation:	For example:
Open Rate	Opened Emails (Unique) / Total Sent Can also be calculated by using the total number of opens, resulting in a higher percentage.	300 opens / 1,000 sent = 30%
Click Through Rate (CTR)	HTML Only: Clicks / Unique Opens HTML, Text, or Both: Total Clicks / Total Sent	15 clicks / 300 opens = 5% 30 clicks / 1,000 sent = 3%
Bounce Rate	Email Returned as Undeliverable / Emails Sent Note: Break this out by hard and soft and, if possible, by type of bounce (i.e., unknown user, mailbox full, and so on.)	10 returned / 1,000 sent = 1%
Capture Rate	List size / Unique Site Visitors	1,000 addresses / 2,000 visitors = 50%
Subscribe Form Completion Rate	Addresses Added to List / Subscribe Form Page Views	1,000 addresses / 2,000 page views = 50%
Unsubscribe Rate	Unsubscribes / List Size Note: To calculate your first issue unsubscribe rate, restrict both numbers to email addresses receiving the email for the first time.	20 unsubscribes / 1,000 addresses = 2%
Block Rate	"Missing" or Bulked Email / Size of Your Seed List	25 missing messages / 250 seed accounts = 10% blocked 50 messages in the "Bulk" or "Junk" folders / 250 seed accounts = 20% blocked Taken together, 30% of your messages didn't get to the inbox.
AOL Complaint Rate	Number of Complaints / Number of Emails Sent to AOL	1 complaint / 2,000 emails sent to AOL = .05%
Internal Complaint Rate	Number of Complaints Received / Number of Emails Sent	1 complaint / 2,000 emails sent = .05%

Measuring the True Impact of Email on Overall Sales

In a truly integrated marketing plan, every ingredient plays a vital role. The fact that you can't directly attribute a sale to every email message doesn't mean the emails aren't working. Response to email is best measured as one part of your whole marketing program.

First, don't be fooled into thinking that email is only a direct-response medium. In fact, there is credible evidence to suggest that email is also effective as a branding medium. A 2004 retailer study by Bigfoot Interactive found that email recipients are 7% more satisfied with purchases than non-recipients. They were also more likely to continue to purchase products from the retailer and to recommend the retailer to others. This suggests that customer satisfaction and loyalty are real and measurable benefits of email marketing that extend beyond the online channel. Even when email is not the direct driver of a particular sale, it has a powerful impact on the recipient's overall brand experience.

The best way to analyze this effect for your company is to examine the behavior of email recipients and non-recipients. Are customers who receive email buying more items, buying more often or spending more? These numbers will truly reveal the long-term impact of your campaigns. You can do this by looking at total purchases, average purchase price and total purchases per year.

You can also dig a layer deeper and measure these sales figures against how long an address has been on your list, their response rates and more. For example, you might discover that a given email address generates a very high open rate but rarely clicks through to purchase. Further investigation, however, reveals that she has total purchases that are 15% higher than average. It would be reasonable to assume that the emails she gets contributes to her spending. The more you can tie your email database to your customer database, the better you will be able to discern correlations between email and selling patterns.

Obviously, digging into this piece of the email equation will go a long way toward making the case for a greater emphasis on the program. It is highly likely that email, combined with other marketing efforts, is making a bigger contribution than many assume.

Remember, too, to look at your web metrics (traffic and sales) in conjunction with your email metrics. First, compare your web metrics on a day you send an email to a day you don't send an email. Be sure you are looking at comparable days (i.e., same day of week, month, year). Also, compare different email campaigns to see if any change in response (open, clicks) correlates to changes in traffic and sales.

Be on the lookout for a rise in traffic without a rise in sales. This may indicate a problem with your landing pages. Also, look for changes in sales in any other channels you may have, such as catalog or retail store sales. If there is a corresponding rise, chances are your email is encouraging them to make a purchase, which they're doing, only through another channel. That's why you should always use promotion codes and special phone numbers for email to track sales through other channels. For retailers with call centers, using a separate phone number in email promotions works well to make the connection between email and sales. In the brick-and-mortar world, printable coupons are an easy way to track the effect email has on store sales.

Email Metrics Troubleshooter

What's Happening:	Possible Cause:
A rise in Web site traffic without a rise in sales	• Poor landing pages • Product/offer problem: promise of email isn't delivered on, price point too high, sale too complicated for email
High sign-up rate, high unsubscribe rate	• Poor or unexpected content
High open rate, low click-through rate	• Offers in your email are not prominent or compelling or aren't relevant to the user
High number of hard bounces	• Old or bad list data
High traffic on Web site, low sign-up rate	• Newsletter invitation on Web site not prominent or compelling • Poor subscription page
High traffic on subscription page, low sign-up rate	• Poor subscription page (e.g.: asking for too much information or irrelevant benefits)
High rate of unsubscribes after first issue	• Poor content • Weak (or no) opt-in • No welcome message
High unsubscribes and/or low opens	• Sending too many emails • Sending without permission of recipient • Irrelevant content
Sudden drop in open rate	• Emails are being blocked by ISPs or other deliverability problems • Subject lines not connecting with audience
Sagging response	• List fatigue • Overmailing • Saturation

Chapter 8: Making Sure Your Messages Make It to the Inbox

Getting delivered to bulk folders is frustrating—especially when you see how many spam messages make it through to your own inbox! But it's a reality you have to address. We track deliverability because the alternative is to discover problems through lower response rates. It's been a smart investment. The program adjustments we've made based on identifying issues were made at virtually no cost. But they provided a dramatic effect on performance. It doesn't pay to hit 'send' and hope for the best.

—Meg Reynolds, manager, email programs, REI, Inc.

Shocking statistic: As much as 50% of all the email you send could be blocked from reaching your recipients—an audience who requested your email in the first place!

Getting your emails delivered is a lot more complicated than just hitting the "send" button. ISP blocking, spam filters, blacklisting, consumer complaints and authentication are just a few of the factors that pose challenges for marketers, but the good news is that you still control many of the levers to deal with them effectively.

Filters: The Inbox Watchdogs

Several times throughout this book, we've bragged about email being the fastest, most far-reaching, cost-effective and interactive form of communication ever created. Thanks to filters, it's also the easiest to validate. While they can present some obstacles for email users and quality marketers alike, filters are a good thing, created to block the unwanted clutter and spam that attempts to invade our inboxes on a daily basis.

In today's environment, ISPs receive a lot of criticism from their customers because of all the spam that evades their filters and makes it to their inboxes. In an attempt to combat this nuisance, the major ISPs (as well as corporate system administrators who manage the mail that comes into business email addresses) are constantly revising their filtering rules to combat spam more effectively. But this is not an exact science, and as we all know, legitimate marketing emails and newsletters have a lot of things in common with spam (spammers make sure of that). Consequently, getting permission-based emails—your emails!—to the inbox is an ongoing challenge.

Deliverability is the foundation of every other email metric used to determine the effectiveness of your campaign. Opens, click-throughs and conversions are directly linked to your ability to deliver email successfully. Every message that is not delivered represents a missed opportunity. Therefore, monitoring and proactively managing deliverability must be a top priority. In part, this requires that you continually address filter and blocking issues. After all, if the greatest ad ever created is never seen by the public, it won't generate an ounce of interest.

In other words, deliverability matters.

Why Your Email Gets Caught by Spam Filters and What to Do about It

Email filters block unwanted email by acting as "online police," constantly scanning for suspicious activity and blocking messages that look or behave like spam. ISPs and corporate system administrators each use a unique suite of filters to create an ever-changing "net" with which they snare most of the spam. Since spammers are constantly trying to get around the nets, ISPs must continually change tactics. Then the mix of filters adjusts to anticipate the next move. It's no wonder your innocent emails get caught, too.

There are filters for content, design, volume, subject lines, domains, the make-up of the list and others. It's usually not one glaring aspect of your email that will get you filtered, it's typically a combination of small infractions that drive your "spam score" high enough to be blocked. Here are some of the incriminating characteristics:

- **Specific words that are typically used by spammers**. Messages containing a combination of these words are either immediately deleted or filed in a "junk" folder that most users never look in. Unfortunately, many of these words are those that any reasonable marketer or publisher would use frequently, such as "free," "discount," "special offer" and "click here." Overcome this hurdle by simply running sample emails through a series of popular message filters to determine your spam score before sending your entire mailing.

- **Gaudy graphics and color combinations.** Many spammers have become infamous for employing such flashy methods to capture the eye, so this is a big red flag to the ISPs. Keep an eye on the graphics-to-text ratio. If you find your design is too "in your face," pull back. After all, good design of relevant content doesn't need to glow in the dark to catch the eye.
- **Very high volume and frequency.** In general, spammers send their garbage emails to a huge number of people at the same time, and they do it very, very, very often. Keep this in mind when determining how much email to send, how to manage volumes over time and how often you send email. Overdoing things may very well work against you. The only way to conquer this is through strict self-control. Just as you need to resist the urge to send self-serving content, resist the desire to send too many emails. Closely monitor how often you mail to each list, and make sure that your subscriber base understands how often they can expect email from you, and *do not* exceed that expectation.

The Other Hobgoblins of Deliverability

Once you've successfully run the gauntlet of filters, you still aren't guaranteed a spot in the inbox. That's because filters aren't a marketer's only obstacles in an email campaign. There are other key areas that every email marketer must pay attention to:

- **Consumer complaints.** You can't make everyone happy all of the time. And unfortunately, someone's definition of spam may be "I'm tired of this" or "This wasn't what I was hoping for." And too often, hitting the "This is spam" button, which registers a complaint to the ISP, often seems easier than unsubscribing. There are two ways to overcome customer complaints. The first is to make your unsubscribe process easier than complaining so unhappy recipients can just delete themselves, without involving the ISP. The second is to maintain excellent relations with ISPs (or outsource this function to a third-party deliverability expert) so you can deal with them directly and prove your ethical business practices by documenting your permission to email the customers who falsely accuse you of spamming. Of course, you should remove any "complainer" from your list immediately. Bottom line: Delight your customers—with both your content and your response to their desire to unsubscribe—and the ISPs will have no reason to block you.

- **Having too many undeliverable emails.** Spammers are notorious for ignoring effective list-building and maintenance techniques. As we just mentioned, they are concerned with high volume, and as a result, they tend to get a lot of emails bounced. Address this problem by continually working to keep your lists clean. Weed out bad addresses (mistyped or bounced as undeliverable) on a regular basis, ideally daily. Be sure to use a validated opt-in followed by a welcome message on sign-up to ensure that good data is coming in. And make it easy for subscribers to change their emails, or use an Email Change of Address service, whenever necessary, so that data stays clean. And if you're purchasing or renting a list, be absolutely sure that the source is reputable and has documentation that the folks on the list have given their permission to receive email. You can learn more about list hygiene in Chapter 5.
- **Sending third-party offers.** Be careful here. While sending third-party offers is not always a bad thing, you must make absolutely sure that your subscribers are aware that you will be doing so. If your subscribers aren't expecting third-party offers, they will think you're spamming them. Make it clear and obvious that these messages are from you and offer the choice of unsubscribing from your third-party offers only—so customers who don't want these messages can still get your newsletter. A better option might be to run ads within your newsletter, rather than sending separate—and potentially unwanted—email.
- **Keeping bad company.** Some email vendors deliver mail for spammers, for unscrupulous marketers or for marketers that do not employ standards and practices at the same level as you. When an ISP sees a high volume of reported spam, they typically block the problematic IP address. However, under certain circumstances, the ISP may also prohibit mail from a block of IP addresses. If your mail goes out from the same server (which is not uncommon), you are "guilty by association" with the problematic mailer. The end result is that even if you are doing everything right, your mail gets blocked. Therefore, it goes without saying that you need to investigate any email delivery service you are considering thoroughly. Even if you use a top-brand email service provider (ESP), if you share a server with other top-brand marketers, you may still run into problems resulting from consumer complaints. The best solution is to insist on an IP address dedicated to your program.

Deliverability Troubleshooter

To Prevent Blocking Because Of:	Be Sure To:
Consumers complaining to their ISPs that you're spamming them	• Make your unsubscribe process easier or more obvious than hitting "This is spam" • Maintain good relations with ISPs so you can prove you're a permission-based marketer • Reconsider any third-party promotional offers you may be sending • Make sure your email delivery service does not send spam from the same IP address from which it sends yours • Use validated opt-in at sign-up
Email that looks or reads like spam	• Eliminate "spam words" such as "free" or "special offer" – especially in the subject line • Avoid garish colors or graphics • Lower the ratio of graphics to text • Check to see that your HTML code is structured correctly
Creeping email volumes or frequency	• Monitor your mailing frequency to each list • Review and adhere to your original mailing frequency agreement with your subscribers
Steadily increasing rate of undeliverable emails	• Use a validated opt-in at sign-up • Keep your list clean and current by using Email List Hygiene and Email Change of Address services

Tracking Deliverability

As we just mentioned, often you don't know if you are being blocked because emails blocked by spam filters don't bounce back to the sender—they simply vanish. From a deliverability perspective, these are the "black holes" of the email world. As a professional and legitimate email marketer, it is your responsibility to watch your list carefully to make sure your outgoing email isn't being diverted to these black holes.

The simplest way to monitor your program deliverability is to watch your numbers. You should be keeping track of your basic metric from mailing to mailing, such as opens and click rate. And while we covered all of these critical metrics in Chapter 7, here's a quick list of things to look for by campaign, and by ISP, that might be a sign your email is being blocked:

- Sudden drops in opens (or clicks for text-only emails)
- Sudden drops in customer response
- Employees don't get emails
- Not receiving emails in your personal account

Unfortunately, even if you do most things right, your emails may still be blocked some of the time. The good news is that there are steps you can take to minimize such blocking:

Break out relevant metrics by ISP

It's hard to notice big dips at one ISP unless you examine your numbers carefully, especially when your list is large. For example, let's say you have a million names on your list and your open rate is 35%. One week your open rate drops to 32%, representing a negative change of 3%. While you may take a look at the elements that contribute to the open rate, you might not be hugely concerned. However, if you discovered that of the 30,000 "missing" opens, 15,000 were all to AOL addresses, which represents 20% of your list, you should be very alarmed. In this scenario, your open rate at AOL had plunged by 21%.

Monitor SMTP log files for deliverability information

SMTP stands for "Simple Mail Transfer Protocol," which is the protocol used for sending email over the internet. If it is enabled, a log is created each time you send or receive email. This data is a goldmine of information. Have someone familiar with email do a quick scan of the logs at regular intervals. By looking for key words in the SMTP logs using a text editor, you can see how the recipient server responds to your delivery attempt.

In most cases, these logs will reveal a combination of successful transmissions, blocked attempts, transient errors, unknown users, receiver system busy responses and so on. The deeper you and your deliverability experts dig, the more you will learn about where your problem areas are and how to address them. Resolving these issues may entail changes to your permission process, your system configuration, your content and design and your list.

Set up test mailboxes

Major ISPs, such as AOL, Yahoo!, MSN/Hotmail, Earthlink, etc., each have their own unique filtering systems. Set up email accounts at each of them, or outsource this monitoring to a deliverability service, and check these accounts every time you send a campaign. For this system to be effective you need several test accounts per ISP (at least ten to fifteen), and they need to be interspersed throughout your database, not clumped together at either the beginning or the end.

Also, you'll want to be sure that the seed accounts are set at varying spam filtering levels, depending on what type of system the ISP uses. For example, some have multiple settings, while others simply have an on/off setting. Finally, you need to check all of these accounts before and after every email campaign. Just because you got delivered yesterday doesn't mean you will get delivered today. If you detect a problem, contact the ISP immediately—it can take days or weeks to get unblocked.

Blacklists and Why They're Bad for Marketers

ISPs block fraudulent email primarily through a system that identifies the IP addresses of the computers that known spammers are using. A list of offending IP addresses that are blocked is called a "blacklist." Once an IP address is on a blacklist, all the email that comes from it is automatically deleted, rejected or dumped into a bulk folder by any ISP or system administrator who subscribes to that blacklist. There are hundreds of blacklists that identify emailers who are suspected spammers, and unfortunately many of the folks who control these lists act as vigilantes, accountable to no one and concerned about their own interests (or whims) rather than good business practices. The most important and reputable ones are Spamhaus, MAPS and SpamCop. Equally important are any technical lists, open relays or open proxies, private ISP blacklists and corporate blacklists (which system administrators may or may not share with you).

To make sure your IP addresses aren't on these blacklists, visit DNS Stuff (http://www.dnsstuff.com) to see if you're on a list. Chances are, whether you send your own email or use an email service, your IP address is on several of these lists at any time. If you find yourself on a list that is significant, you need to negotiate your way off of it by adjusting your practices and communicating effectively with the list owner. If you find yourself on minor blacklists, typically run by individuals with an axe to grind and very little influence in the marketplace, you may be best served to ignore it. We recommend you continue to check all your IP addresses regularly.

Lessons from the Inbox:
The Art of ISP Relations

If you find yourself on an ISP's blacklist, it's going to take more than a quick phone call and a heartfelt "I'm sorry, please give me another chance" to get off of that list. You need to prove that you are indeed an ethical marketer by providing the ISP with documented proof that you are on the up-and-up. A solid history with very few black marks helps a lot. Another critical defense is the permission of your subscribers, so the ISP understands that you were invited to send these folks email. In addition, a mailing schedule that demonstrates that you are adhering to your agreed-upon mailing frequency goes a long way toward proving you're not violating any agreements with your subscribers.

As in any professional relationship, however, the best business practice is to establish a rapport with all of the major ISPs from the start—before you have a problem. Of course, there are tens of thousands of permission mailers and usually fewer than half a dozen postmasters or security representatives at even the larger ISPs. The sheer numbers illustrate that it is impossible for every marketer to have a personal relationship with the ISPs. If you are a large mailer, you can arrange regular meetings with their compliance personnel to make sure that they understand your approach to permission-based email marketing and that you're up on their latest policies and procedures. If you are a smaller mailer, you may need to enlist the help of a third-party expert. This way, if a negative scenario arises, you've already established a level of familiarity with the ISP and demonstrated your willingness to follow best practices, both of which make issue resolution considerably easier.

Whitelists and Why They're Good for Marketers

While ISPs are constantly working to improve their filtering capabilities, there is a way to help ensure that your emails avoid getting snared in their filters. It's called "whitelisting." Unfortunately, it's not a panacea: making it onto a whitelist does not mean that you can ignore all the other best practices around deliverability. (In fact, ignoring those rules will get you kicked off of the whitelist.) Whitelist inclusion will, however, help establish your reputation as an ethical email marketer and, for most, improve the deliverability of your emails.

There are two types of "large-scale" whitelists that you can be a part of. The first is an individual ISP's whitelist. After applying for whitelist status, the ISP reviews aspects of your program and practices and determines whether or not to add you to their whitelist. If you are accepted into their whitelist program, your mail will generally be delivered, barring any filter triggers and provided that your mailing list is clean and your mail does not generate excessive consumer complaints. Of the major ISPs, only AOL and Yahoo! currently have active whitelisting programs.

The second type of large-scale whitelist is a third-party whitelist, such as Bonded Sender. Generally, you pay to participate in a third-party whitelisting program. As with ISP whitelists, you must meet established criteria to participate in the program. Providers of third-party whitelists have agreements with ISPs and corporate administrators to use the whitelist to identify legitimate senders.

And when you've found yourself on one of the large-scale whitelists, continually monitor your status to make sure you're staying in the inbox.

Personal whitelists: an individual invitation to an inbox

The third type of whitelist is a personal whitelist, also known as the "Address Book." Though it is individual, it may be just as important as the first two. The personal whitelist gives recipients ultimate control over what gets delivered to their inboxes by allowing them to create a list of companies and publishers from whom they want to receive mail. The best way to ensure that your messages get delivered to the inboxes of your subscribers is to get into their Address Book. It goes without saying, then, that you should take advantage of every opportunity to encourage your subscribers/customers to add you to their "known sender" or "people I know" whitelists or address books.

We recommend a six-step program to encourage personal whitelisting:

1. Promote whitelisting at sign-up by providing specific instructions. We've used a free tool called CleanMyMailbox (http://www.cleanmymailbox.com/whitelist.html) to help many clients get started.

2. Include whitelisting instructions in the welcome message you send to new subscribers.

3. Send a one-time email to existing list members, similar to the welcome message, that encourages them to whitelist you and includes instructions. It's a good idea to repeat this exercise for your full list once or twice a year.

4. Add whitelisting instructions to the text link you include at the top of your HTML emails. Including this link is important if the recipient's email reader does not allow graphics, either for some emails or only for select ones, and the space it occupies can easily promote address book inclusion, too. The copy should read something like, "Make sure you always get these emails by adding our company to your address book. If you cannot view this email message, visit here." That browser page should include a call to action to whitelist and instructions on doing so, since this will often help to prevent problems with graphics in future emails, too. You should include this information in every email you send.

5. Use a consistent "From" address. There is evidence that some email servers are only concerned with domain (so if "newsletter@company.com" is on the list, then "order@company.com" will also get through), but it is unclear if this is universally true. To be safe, we recommend you use one "From" address for all email communications (including customer service, order confirmations, marketing and welcome). The key is for the actual "From" address to be consistent. The words (or alias) that appear in the customers' email client as the "From" name can be adjusted to suit the content—Editor or Order Confirmation or Customer Service.

6. If a recipient on AOL 9.0 replies to your message, you are automatically added to the whitelist for graphics and links (though not, unfortunately, for delivery), so it is worth encouraging your AOL customers to reply to one of your messages.

An important point to keep in mind is that personal whitelisting does not guarantee deliverability. If your IP address is on the ISP's blacklist, or if your email scores high on the filters' spam scale, your email will not be allowed through, no matter how many address books you're in.

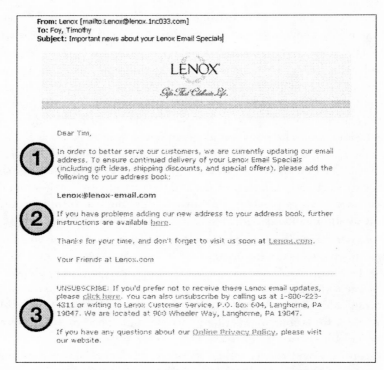

A great way to encourage your subscribers to add you to their address book is to send them a special email like the one shown here by Lenox. They offer a compelling reason for doing so (1), provide a link for instructions for those less technically savvy (2) and, of course, include prominent unsubscribe instructions and privacy statements (3). This is an effective way to improve the deliverability of future emails.

Authentication: How ISPs Tell the Good Guys from the Bad Guys

ISPs are working hard to create new and better ways to distinguish the good guys from the spammers, thus making it easier for them to block unwanted email. Authentication is a key component in the ISP's broad approach to stopping spam. It is part of the "proof" they look for to identify good senders, along with reputation services and accreditation.

Quite simply, authentication is a way for the ISP to verify the identity of the sender. If the identity of the sender cannot be validated, ISPs may reject or alter the message. ISPs are expanding their authentication rules because spammers often forge, or "spoof," identities to shield themselves and make it harder for ISPs, blacklists, the government and others to catch them.

Major ISPs have already begun to implement authentication programs, and cooperating with them is mandatory for any marketer or sender who wishes to remain on the ISP's whitelist and ensure high deliverability of email. Unfortunately, each set of authentication requirements is different, though the ISPs have taken two general approaches to authentication:

- **IP-based: SPF and Sender ID**. These approaches require publishing text records in the Domain Name Service (DNS) record for every one of your domains. Messages from a certain domain will then be authenticated by comparing the IP address of the server that is actually sending the message (which is really difficult to spoof) to the list of IP addresses that are permitted to send for that domain. The difference between the two standards primarily concerns which domain is authenticated. In general, SPF authenticates the envelope "From" address (this is the address the receiving email server sees). In most typical implementations, Sender ID will authenticate on the "header from" (also called "body from") address (the one the final recipient sees in their email application).
- **Cryptographic: DomainKeys**. This approach requires that each message contain a "signature" that is impossible to forge, proving that the message came from the purported sending domain.

Consider This: Be a "White Hat" Sender

ISPs have pledged to work together on a standard. But for the short term there will be multiple sets of requirements for marketers who want to continue to ensure their program deliverability. Follow the rules mandated by the major ISPs, corporate system administrators and the government to ensure that your reputation as an email marketer is untarnished. This is the absolute best way to keep your standing as one of the good guys, to ensure you are a "white hat" sender.

WARNING: The Rules Are Changing All the Time

At press time, there was still significant debate among the larger ISPs as to which of these standards would be adopted, on what timeframes and to what degree.

Because there is no industry standard yet, there is no silver bullet, no one system to meet the various requirements. But there are some practical steps that every marketer should take to ensure participation.

Since the specifications from the ISPs are still in motion, here is our best advice:

- Work with your IT group or ESP to gather the information required to publish SPF, Sender-ID and Domain Key records.
- Make sure you publish records for *every* IP address in use at your company—including transactional, customer service, corporate, sales and marketing emails as well as those used by outside ESPs that send mail from their IP address on behalf of your company and use your domain in the "From" address. You may have different IT teams involved in each of these areas.
- Coordinate with major ISPs to ensure you're compliant with their specifications.
- Be prepared to adjust as the landscape changes. Considering how rapidly the landscape does change, it would be wise to consult with deliverability experts.

Lessons from the Inbox: Hiring and Working with an Email Service Provider

Email Service Providers, or ESPs, often argue that their ability to deliver email makes them a superior choice to a sending email in-house. If using an ESP is right for your company, you'll want to be sure they are doing everything right from a deliverability and accountability standpoint and that there is transparency to the process.

We've created a list of criteria that you should consider when choosing your partner:

- **Proactive deliverability monitoring.** ESPs have varying degrees of success getting your email delivered. Ask for documentation that proves their success rates, keeping in mind that no one is at 100%, and make sure that they have staff and technology that are committed to monitoring the problem by performing critical functions such as mapping SMTP log files for response codes and reporting domain blocking, bounce causes (both hard and soft), blacklists and unknown user rates.

- **Technical assistance with your data.** If you already have your own list or lists, be sure that your ESP can assist with your initial data upload. Depending on the size of the file, this can be a slow and complex process, so you want to be sure that there is an expert on their side to be sure the data transfers correctly. Additionally, if you are planning on uploading new lists every time you mail, you want to make sure the host can handle this process smoothly. And be sure they are able to assist you with list hygiene and maintenance by using hygiene services with every file upload. Lastly, be sure that all of this data is always synchronized with your company-wide Do-Not-Email list.

- **A quality backup system.** Your data is precious, so be absolutely sure that your ESP has regular and extensive backup procedures in place. Know how to get a copy of your backup in case of emergency and download your own backup copy of your lists on a weekly basis, at the very least. This is valuable data—you don't want the only copy of your list to sit on another company's server.

- **Easy-to-use system administration features.** Most ESPs use web interfaces that allow their clients to access the system to upload lists, launch campaigns and monitor day-to-day administration information such as open rates, etc. While features have become very similar across the various ESPs, be sure that you and your team select one that you all feel comfortable using.

- **Quality ISP relations.** It's important that your ESP is viewed as professional and ethical by ISPs. Make sure that they have a staff dedicated to working with ISPs to maintain this standing to ensure maximum deliverability and resolve any problems that may arise, including blacklisting, blocking and filtering. And don't be afraid to ask for references at various ISPs so you can verify this information.

- **A dedicated IP address.** You always want your own IP address so that your deliverability is affected only by your own actions. Some ESPs charge extra for this, but it's worth the cost. Factor this fee into your overall assessment of the value of the services being offered.

- **The ability to mail at different rates to different domains.** Volume cap filters are common at certain ISPs. The standards change frequently, so be sure that your ESP can keep up with how the various ISPs handle volume and make quick adjustments to work in accordance with ISP volume triggers.

- **Customer service/abuse queue handling.** Responding to email complaints can be a time-consuming task. As we discussed in Chapter 5, it's critical to have a real live person perform this task. Some ESPs can do it for you, so just make sure they follow custom directions from you about how to handle different kinds of complaints properly and report back to you regularly on the topic.

- **Message content review and assistance.** Some of the better ESPs will have experts on staff who can review the various aspects of your content in advance and provide quality recommendations for improvement. Request an advance check of your email content and subject lines to be sure they pass the most widely used client and server side spam filters.

- **A good reputation.** You've worked hard to be a high-quality marketer; don't have your email blocked because your ESP does most of its work for spammers. Select some of their IP addresses and run them against the major blacklists using DNS Stuff (http://www.dnsstuff.com) or SpamCop (http://www.spamcop.com) and see what shows up. If they are on a few minor blacklists, don't worry—everyone is. If they are on a lot of minor blacklists, be wary. If they are on a major blacklist, find another vendor.

- **Try before you buy.** Before you select an ESP, ask for a trial account. Have several members of your team perform the basic functions, such as creating a list, sending a message, handling an unsubscribe, etc. These are the tasks you are going to be performing every day, and if they aren't easy and intuitive, you should look elsewhere.

The Keys to Ensuring Maximum Deliverability

As we mentioned earlier, on average, 20% of all permission-based email does not get delivered by ISPs, and many marketers see up to 50% of their mail not showing up in their customers' inboxes. Thankfully, this is mostly preventable, as you have control over many of the factors affecting whether your email reaches the inbox, but you must take action on the issue of deliverability. Don't limit yourself to pressing "send" and hoping for the best. Be proactive and follow the key chapters outlined thus far. And whether you're handling your own mailing or using an ESP, keep these critical practices in mind:

Monitor all of the key elements that affect delivery, filtering, blocking and blacklisting

You want to make sure you have a comprehensive system in place to monitor and provide reports for all mail, sent by any server, either in-house or at your ESP, so you can

- create baseline reports for mail sent by ESP.
- track blocked email messages.
- track messages sent to bulk mail.
- track messages accepted for delivery.
- track messages sent to top ISPs, such as AOL, MSN/Hotmail and Yahoo!, as well as those sent to secondary ISPs, such as NetZero, Earthlink, Verizon and RoadRunner.
- respond to email complaints in a timely, professional manner.
- review timely data. This will give you the ability to assess and resolve potential issues proactively.

Analyze the results and data to uncover and resolve issues

Expert diagnostics and analysis can help you uncover and fix the root causes of complaints, blocking, filtering and blacklisting, so make sure that you

- get a pre-campaign Pass/Fail rating on major client and server side filters so you can accurately predict your spam score.
- review all content and design templates to remove any negative impacts on delivery performance.
- practice list hygiene, reviewing for spam trap addresses, stale data, bad addresses, bounces and troublesome role accounts.

- periodically re-examine your permission practices.
- evaluate your unsubscribe process for ease of use (and be sure it really works!).
- review and analyze all complaint data on a timely basis.

Resolve all ISP issues promptly and professionally

ISPs are the gatekeepers to your prospects and customers, so be sure to treat them with courtesy, respect and a high degree of professionalism. You can demonstrate this behavior by

- handling all customer complaints in a timely manner and taking steps to address glaring concerns.
- dealing promptly with alerts that you or your ESP has appeared on major and minor blacklists.
- encouraging whitelisting on both the ISP and personal levels.
- assigning dedicated staff to work with ISPs to resolve all issues promptly and maintain good standing.

Optimize your practices and systems to overcome difficult obstacles

Proactive, systemic review will go a long way toward removing obstacles and optimizing all aspects of your program. That said, be sure to

- keep a scorecard of your email performance. This will allow you to create accurate benchmarks.
- conduct regular reviews of your program to stay ahead off any potential problems.
- constantly review and refine your systems to stay ahead of the curve on key issues, such as volume control to different ISPs.

Chapter 9: CAN-SPAM and Other Email Legislation

Before CAN-SPAM went into effect, we worked with our legal department to thoroughly review our email program and made several changes to ensure compliance. While compliance was our primary objective, we also saw this as an opportunity to reassure consumers that Lenox sends legitimate, permission-based email. For that reason, we actually went beyond the requirements of the law. For example, we now include our 800 number and a privacy policy link in all of our messages.

—Timothy Foy, assistant marketing manager, Lenox

We've been mentioning it over and over throughout this book: CAN-SPAM—the first federal legislation designed to tame the Wild West of email marketing. It sets a standard of decorum for anyone who sends email for promotional purposes, one that not only outlines minimum standards of decency for direct marketers but holds those who violate the rules legally accountable for their actions.

For ethical marketers like us, CAN-SPAM—and other legislation like it—creates a few hurdles but also a tremendous opportunity. Before we get into how to leverage the opportunity, let's start with the basics.

All about CAN-SPAM Compliance

When the CAN-SPAM Act of 2003 (the acronym stands for "Controlling the Assault of Non-Solicited Pornography and Marketing") took effect on January 1, 2004, it gave bulk commercial emailers—marketers, publishers and ebillers—a whole new set of email standards. If you're a legitimate email marketer, this is great news, since it will make things tougher on spammers. But it's important that you are aware of every step you must take to be compliant with the CAN-SPAM Act.

Under CAN-SPAM, companies that send emails for marketing purposes **must** *do the following:*

- Include a viable internet-based opt-out mechanism, which must be active for a minimum of thirty days after you send the emails. The law does not specify what type of internet-based opt-out mechanism, so you can use what works best for your company.
- Stop sending unsolicited advertisements or solicitations to anyone opting out by processing all unsubscribe requests within ten days.
- Display the physical address of your company within the body of the email.
- Include a clear and conspicuous announcement that the email is an advertisement or solicitation either in the subject line or in the content of the email.
- Clearly label any emails that contain sexually explicit material. In fact, the law includes very specific provisions for dealing with this type of material. If you are sending this type of content we would strongly urge you to seek legal counsel to ensure compliance.

Under CAN-SPAM, companies that send emails for marketing purposes **cannot** *do the following:*

- Use a false or misleading "From" line.
- Use a subject line that masks the purpose of the email.
- Harvest email addresses off the internet, which means to randomly collect publicly-available email addresses, such as those available on many company web sites, posting boards or weblogs ("blogs").
- Launch dictionary attacks, which means using software that guesses email addresses by randomly creating logical name and domain combinations. For example, asmith@hotmail.com, bsmith@hotmail.com, csmith@hotmail.com and—well, you get the idea.

While most experts (and marketers) agree that the CAN-SPAM legislation will not solve the spam problem, it is a great first step towards giving the federal government the authority to prosecute the most egregious spammers. And contrary to the opinions of some, who think that government regulation means the death of legitimate commercial email, the CAN-SPAM Act will help legitimate email marketers by making fraudulent and deceptive email practices punishable by fines and jail time.

Additional Legislation You Need to Know about: The California Online Privacy Protection Act

In addition to CAN-SPAM, there's a new law on the books in California that requires all marketers who collect personal information online from California consumers to have a privacy policy, prominently display it and ensure it contains specific information.

The California Online Privacy Protection Act of 2003 (referred to as OPPA), states that if you have any California residents on your email list or if you offer ecommerce to California consumers, your privacy policy must be prominently displayed. We recommend that it be linked from the footer on every page of your web site, wherever you collect email addresses or any personal information, such as "My Account" areas and subscribe forms, and also above the fold on your homepage. For your home or primary ecommerce pages, the footer may not be visible enough.

The law also requires that your policy contain the following information:

- A list of the categories of information collected anywhere on your site.
- A list of the categories of third parties with whom you may share the information. If you don't share information, we recommend you state that specifically.
- A description of what, if anything, a consumer can do to review and change their personal information.
- A description of how you notify consumers of changes to your policy.
- The effective date of your policy, which we recommend putting at the top of the page.

As the law is tested in the marketplace and the courts, more specific compliance may become available. In addition, you may begin to see other states adopt similar legislation to protect their citizens, so stay on top of these issues! For the most up to date information on legislation affecting email marketing, visit our web site at www.returnpath.biz/signmeup.

READER TAKE HEED!

Here is one last—and most important—point regarding all of the legal issues referenced herein. We are not lawyers, nor do we claim to represent you legally on matters that involve your email efforts. All the insights and recommendations we provide in this book are meant to serve as a guideline and are based on our informed interpretation of the laws. It is not intended as a substitute for your own thorough review of the laws. It's always wise to consult with your own counsel on ways to ensure your own organization is compliant.

Going Beyond the Letter of the Law

We said in the beginning of this chapter that legislation can create an opportunity for marketers. That's because consumers are looking for compliance from companies to whom they give permission to email. This gives you the opportunity to erase even the appearance of "spamminess" from all of your practices and all of the emails that you send. You can achieve this by complying with the spirit of the law, not just the letter of the law, to take advantage of consumer perceptions about what makes a "white hat" sender and what looks like spam.

How? By following the guidelines of this book, of course! And by going beyond what the law demands:

- Respecting unsubscribes immediately, not just within ten days.
- Never sending email to anyone who does not specifically request it from you (or your trusted third-party partner).
- Keeping your list clean and well maintained.
- Following strict, consumer-friendly permission practices. Double opt-in, which requires affirmative confirmation of opt-in, is the highest permission standard.
- Clearly stating your privacy policy in plain language—not legal jargon—and doing so in an obvious manner, as well.
- Monitoring and attending to your deliverability to ensure your emails always make it to the inbox.
- Ensuring that the content and design of your emails do not trigger spam filters or the ire of your customers.
- Avoiding even the perception of spam to increase the likelihood that your emails are indeed welcomed, opened, read and acted upon.

And that's not legal advice either. It's just good business sense.

Part III Optimization Strategies: Summary

- Email allows for fast, dynamic testing, because it provides almost instantaneous feedback from recipients, so there's no reason not to test some element before almost every mailing.

- The main aspects of your email that you should test often are subject lines, offer sequence and placement, number of offers, mailing frequency, content length and order, landing pages and design.

- Continually request feedback from your subscribers by using surveys and other techniques. This is the best way to test your newsletter's continuing relevance.

- When testing the success of your email campaigns, watch these metrics: opens, clicks, bounces, number of emails captured and subscription-form completion rate.

- Take your analysis to the next level by digging into the metrics that reveal the number of customers that you anger with email and the percentage of your messages that never get delivered due to email filtering.

- As much as 50% of the email you send that is blocked by email filters may not be bounced and returned but simply deleted by the ISP. Is it imperative that you monitor and understand your true deliverability rate. (Hint, it is much more complex than the number of emails that bounce.)

- Things that will get your email blocked include words that are typically used by spammers, such as "free," "discount," "special offer" and "click here"; gaudy graphics and color combinations; very high volume and frequency; too many undeliverable emails and the use of an ESP that also sends email for spammers.

- Blacklists are listings of the IP addresses used by known spammers or email abusers. Once an IP is on a blacklist, all the email from there is automatically deleted by servers employing that blacklist.

- Whitelists are lists of companies and publishers from whom emails are usually accepted. Whitelists can be created by individuals for their own email inboxes, by ISPs for their entire network, and by "third-party" companies, who, for a fee from those included on the whitelist, work to promote their own whitelists to various ISPs.

- If hosting your own list is not feasible for your company, you can out-source the function to an email service provider, but be sure they meet your standards and can provide the exact level and types of services you require.

- CAN-SPAM is the first legislation of its kind, holding marketers responsi-ble for the material that they send via email. Among the highlights of the legislation is the requirement to process all unsubscribe requests within ten days, to display the physical address of the company within the body of the email and to include an obvious announcement that the email is a solicitation. In addition, CAN-SPAM makes it illegal to use a false or mis-leading "From" address, a subject line that masks the purpose of the email, email addresses "harvested" off the internet and "dictionary" attacks.

- Even with the new laws, it's in your best interest to go beyond the law to prove your ethical conduct as a marketer. This type of behavior will go a long way toward building trust among ISPs and email recipients—and building the all-important solid business reputation.

Afterword: The Future of Email

We've heard over and over from various pundits about how email is on the way out and that we'll soon be back to the trusty pad and pencil. Email will certainly die an early death, they say, because there are too many issues with viruses, spam, IT management costs and employment practices. Email is close to having a bigger downside than upside, they claim, and will eventually go the way of the typewriter and the floppy disk drive. Still and again we hear from so-called marketing and industry "experts" who claim that email is not a viable marketing medium, since most users prefer not to have marketing messages of any kind delivered to their inboxes.

Nonsense.

Email is alive and well, and it will surely continue to be one of the most powerful media—for personal, business and marketing uses—of all time. And here's why:

People are signing up for email newsletters and marketing at astonishing rates

If email was indeed on the way out, this is the single metric you'd expect to be falling. Well, guess what? This metric is on the rise! Our company alone is getting almost 80,000 people each day to sign up for our various email-related services. And a recent story in *Internet Retailer* highlighted a program launched by Home Depot. They started a Garden Club, complete with newsletters targeted by region. In just twenty-four hours it had more than 25,000 sign-ups! The list quickly grew to 90,000, and they are proving to be an active club with many writing in with questions on gardening. What's more, many companies who sell direct to consumers online are generating upwards of 25% of their revenue via email. These are not exactly the signs of a dying—or even slightly ill—medium.

Consumer use of email and the internet for purchasing goods is widespread and rising

Research backs up this claim. The Direct Marketing Association, in its "State of E-Commerce Report" for 2004, indicated that email marketing to house lists is the most used online marketing method. And it works. A recent Travel Industry

Association report revealed that more than 35 million online travelers have signed up with a travel supplier web site or online travel service to receive email offers and promotions and that nearly a third of them (10 million, to be precise) have been influenced by an email promotion to actually take a trip they otherwise would not have taken!

Email business usage is now critical for most employees

Economic productivity gains from email usage are almost incalculable. For a quick flashback, compare the time spent firing off an email to five members of your team, cc'ing two other colleagues, and bcc'ing your boss to keep everyone in the loop to the painstaking analog tasks of making phone calls, holding meetings and writing then distributing a paper memo. There's simply no comparison, and every successful business person knows it.

Technology to block spam is getting better every day

While there is still a cat-and-mouse game going on between spammers and spam filters that will always result in a certain amount of false positives (good email that gets filtered) or false negatives (true spam that sneaks past the filter), technology is progressing to the point where this problem will soon be inconsequential. In fact, the Anti-Spam Technical Alliance, an industry group that includes AOL, Yahoo, EarthLink, Comcast, British Telecom and Microsoft—companies that provide a large majority of the world's email inboxes—have joined forces to endorse a set of anti-spam best practices for email service providers and large senders. These major industry players have dedicated themselves to work together toward creating new technologies that will make it much more difficult to be a spammer.

Email drives revenue

Internet Retailer reported that on average email generates $15.50 in sales per dollar spent. That translates to 17% more than direct mail. Meanwhile, the cost to send email to customers has fallen to between $0.03 and $0.05 per email. With email you spend less per piece and get more. That's an equation any marketer can love!

Email enhances the effectiveness of other marketing efforts

With the rapid growth of high-speed internet connections and the popularity of handheld email devices and internet cafes, it goes without saying that email has become a major part of today's society. And with so many people spending so much time and effort using email, these folks are obviously spending less time with other media, such as TV, radio and newspapers. Smart marketers must stake their claim in this space or risk being left behind. In addition to the new opportunities it offers to reach prospects and customers, email as part of the marketing mix reinforces your branding efforts across all media and magnifies your other marketing expenditures.

Here's the plain and simple truth: ignoring email as a marketing vehicle is ignoring consumer behavior. In about ten short years, email has become completely ingrained in our society and in our communication patterns. In fact, email as a communication medium is now much less about the technology than about human interaction and habit. Heck, in our office alone, we've got someone with a three-year-old niece and another person with a ninety-two-year-old grandmother, both of whom use email (for those keeping track, that's an eighty-nine-year age gap).

It's great to be a marketer! We live in a remarkable time, with access to the fastest, most cost-effective and interactive form of communication ever created: email. It reaches to the ends of the world and back again, and it does it in milliseconds. It's as fundamentally powerful as the telephone, only it does what telephones can't—carry important packages in the form of documents, pictures and, for our purposes, requested marketing information. And as the technology that builds and shapes email changes and improves on a daily basis, the email phenomenon will only become more compelling for marketers as new opportunities arise.

And better yet, your customers will ask you for it. When someone says, "Sign me up to your newsletter" and gives you her email address voluntarily, she is essentially saying, "Sell me something, please." You can't get a better marketing opportunity than that.

So what are you waiting for?

Get out there and start using email to build your brands, forge your presence and boost sales. You can do it. It's easier than you think. As long as you stick to the rules, especially the first one—always get permission to send email—you'll do just fine.

Be sure to let us know how it goes. We want to hear from you, and we'll share your experiences with other readers if you like. Visit our web site at www.returnpath.biz/signmeup or email us at signmeup@returnpath.net.

How to Stay Current on the Latest Email Trends and Techniques

Email is perhaps the most dynamic media in existence. As such, keeping up with the pace isn't easy. In fact, there are times when ideas shared or opinions expressed regarding email are written down only to be outdated before the ink is even dry. That said, we've created an online resource where you can go to keep current on all of the key elements of this book, including

- full-color screen shots from the book, plus more examples,
- the most up to date legal issues regarding email compliance,
- cutting-edge ideas for content and design,
- the latest trends on list building
- and more!

So keep your email newsletter skills honed by visiting
www.returnpath.biz/signmeup

Glossary

A

Accreditation-based systems: Third-party whitelist programs, such as Bonded Sender from IronPort or Trusted Sender from Habeas, that aim to convince ISPs that those using the systems are legitimate mailers who should never be blocked.

Authentication: The practice by ISPs and other mail gateway administrators to establish the true identity of the sender. Examples of proposed authentication standards include DomainKeys (Yahoo), SPF (PO Box, AOL), Caller ID for email or Sender ID (Microsoft) and dot.mail.

B

Blacklist, public: A list of IP addresses believed to send spam. Created and held by third parties; sometimes used by ISPs as another filtering mechanism to block email delivery.

Blacklist, private: A list of IP addresses believed to send spam, compiled by an ISP based on user complaints, mail sent to spam trap addresses and unknown user rates. Used to block email delivery.

Bounce: A message sent by a receiving system that "bounces back" to the originating server to alert the sender of the non-delivery.

Bulk mail folder: Folder within email clients to which questionable email is often directed. Also referred to as "Junk" or "Spam" folders in some email clients.

Blackhole: Term describing what happens to email that is blocked without a bounce response to the sender.

C

Caller ID for Email: Proposed way to help block spam and spoofing attacks by asking the IP address sending email whether the domain it represents is legitimate. Compares the "From" address and content to the IP address authorized to send the email. Proposed by Microsoft.

CAN-SPAM: Federal legislation governing unsolicited commercial email that went into effect on January 1, 2004. This law does not prohibit unsolicited commercial email, but it does regulate how it must be sent. Lawmakers intended to protect the end user and to make prosecution of spammers easier. The acronym stands for "Controlling the Assault of Non-Solicited Pornography and Marketing."

Challenge Response: Method of approving senders to specific email addresses that asks the email sender to answer a question proving he is a real person and not a spam machine attempting to send email. Primarily used by Earthlink and selected client-side filters.

Commercial email: Marketing or sales oriented email that is sent in bulk.

Confirmed opt-in: A process where a subscriber opts in to your newsletter and then receives an email message confirming their subscription and offering them the option to immediately unsubscribe if the subscription was in any way a mistake. Unlike double opt-in, the receiver does not have to take any action in order to be added to the list.

Content filters: Software filters that block email based on words, phrases or header information within the email itself. Goal is to identify and filter to the Bulk or Junk mail folders any email that is likely to be spam.

D

Delivery monitoring: A process, usually using third-party tools and techniques, to measure true delivery rates by campaign and ISP. Also tracks amount and type of email tagged and/or blocked by server and client-side filters.

Dictionary attack: Type of spam program that bombards a mail server with millions of alphabetically-generated email addresses in the hope that some addresses will be guessed correctly.

Domain: Internet addresses made up of words that correspond to the Internet Protocol (IP) numbers computers use to find each other. Domains always have two or more parts, separated by "dots."

DomainKeys: Email-authentication system proposed by Yahoo! that requires each message to be "signed" cryptographically. This would make messages impossible to spoof and prove that they came from the purported sending domain.

Double opt-in: The process that double-checks the desire to be included on an email list after a primary registration. Typically done via an email that requires a non-automated response (proof that a live person is at the other end of the email address) in order for the email address to be added to the list. Also called confirmed or verified opt-in.

DNS: Domain Name System translates domain names into an IP address to find the owner's site.

E

Email delivery rates: The percentage of email that gets delivered as intended; compiled from seedlist-based monitoring services and SMTP log files.

ECOA: Email Change of Address. Process that provides updated email addresses for data files based on consumer-provided, permission-based data.

Email append: Process that adds email addresses to postal files by merging files to match the postal address against email information in other files.

ESP: An Email Solutions Provider is a company that sends and manages email campaigns for companies that use email to communicate with customers.

F

False negative: When spam-filtering devices fail to detect spam and allow it to be delivered.

False positive: When spam-filtering devices inaccurately identify legitimate email as spam.

G

Graylisting: Process of routing email to a bulk folder if it is borderline spam in eyes of ISPs. Next step is blacklisting, which blocks the email altogether.

H

Harvesting: Scanning the internet to identify email addresses and uses them to create lists for spamming.

Header: The first part of an email message, which contains controlling data and metadata such as the subject, origin and destination email addresses, the path an email takes, and its priority. May be used to filter, track spammers or uncover information about delivery rates.

I

IP addresses: The numeric identification number that refers to a specific machine on the internet.

Internet Service Provider (ISP): Company that provides access to the internet through connectivity services. Examples include AOL, Comcast, Earthlink and Verizon.

L

List hygiene: Process of cleaning email files to ensure all addresses are accurate and deliverable.

M

Machine-learning filters: Filters run by machines that determine whether to block email based on algorithms that identify likely spam messages.

O

Open relay: SMTP email server that allows the third-party relay of email messages through the SMTP "port" on a server (port 25). While this feature of SMTP servers has legitimate uses, spammers have learned how to locate unprotected servers and use them to send spam.

Open proxy: Software that exists on a server that allows the third-party relay of email messages through ports other than port 25.

Opt-in: Process of agreeing to receive email from a business source. Confirmed opt-in refers to a double-check procedure in which a decision to be included on a mailing list is confirmed.

Opt-out: Process of declining to receive email from a business source or unsubscribing if the recipient is already on a mailing list.

P

Phishing: (Pronounced 'fishing') A replica of a legitimate web page that tries to trick users into submitting personal or financial information or passwords.

Postmaster: The person who manages mail servers at an organization. Usually the one to contact at a particular server/site to get help or information or to log complaints.

R

Rich media: A web technology creating an interactive atmosphere for viewers online through things such as streaming video and audio files.

S

Seed list: A list of email addresses that should be included in every email event to monitor delivery across email platforms. Can be done in house or through a third-party vendor.

SPF: Email authentication process used by AOL (on outbound mail) that prevents domain forgery.

SMTP: Simple Mail Transfer Protocol, a server-to-server protocol used to transfer email between computers.

SMTP log file: A file showing all conversations back and forth between servers during the email send-and-receive process. Used to uncover problems with various deliverability factors such as unknown user rates.

Spam: Widely-used slang reference to unsolicited commercial email messages. Named after the popular Monty Python "Spam" sketch and song.

Spam filter: Systems that watch for spam and block it before it can hit the inbox. Spam filters can be complaint or content based.

Spam-trap address: An email address that is set up specifically to catch people who are harvesting addresses or using directory attacks to send unsolicited email. Used by Brightmail, ISPs and many in the anti-spam community.

Spoofing: Forged email addresses that hide the origin of a spam or virus message. Used to trick people into opening an email in the belief that it has come from a legitimate source.

Suppression list: A list of email addresses that should not be mailed to any longer (kept by a single organization). Usually owners of the addresses on the list have specifically requested inclusion. Required by CAN-SPAM.

U

Unknown User: Bounce error code generated by an ISP when an email address is not registered in its system.

V

Verified opt-in: The process of verifying opt-in by requiring that the recipient perform an action before being added to the list. More commonly known as double opt-in.

W

Whitelist: A list of trusted IP addresses and domains that allows all mail from these addresses to be delivered, bypassing spam filters.

Resource Guide

Throughout this book, we've mentioned lots of web sites in our examples of good marketing practices, or as valuable resources for your own efforts. To make things convenient, they're all listed below. Visit them. Bookmark them. Sign up for their emails and see for yourself what works in email marketing.

Marketers
Amazon.com: www.amazon.com
American Management Association: www.amanet.org
Barnes & Noble: www.barnesandnoble.com
Beechnut: www.beechnut.com
Blue Mountain Arts: www.bluemountain.com
Business & Legal Reports: www.blr.com
DailyCandy: www.dailycandy.com
EasyAsk: www.easyask.com
eBay: www.ebay.com
Fast Company: www.fastcompany.com
Good Experience: www.goodexperience.com
iVillage: www.ivillage.com
Jeep: www.jeep.com
Kimberly Clark: www.kcprofessional.com/us/
Krispy Kreme: www.krispykreme.com
Lenox: www.lenox.com
Lifeway Christian Resources: www.lifeway.com
MarketingSherpa: www.marketingsherpa.com
Military.com: www.military.com
REI: www.rei.com
Subscriber Mail: www.subscribermail.com
YouThink.Com: www.youthink.com

Blacklists:
Spamhaus: www.spamhaus.org
MAPS: www.mail-abuse.com
SpamCop: www.spamcop.com

Third-Party Whitelists:
Habeas: www.habeas.com
BondedSender: www.bondedsender.com

Tools:
DNS Stuff: http://www.dnsstuff.com
CleanMyMailbox: www.cleanmymailbox.com/whitelist.html

Feedback Loops:
AOL: http://postmaster.info.aol.com/fbl/index.html
United Online: www.unitedonline.net/postmaster/whitelisted.html
SpamCop: www.spamcop.net/fom-serve/cache/94.html
Abuse.net: www.abuse.net/addnew.html

About Return Path

Return Path strives to make permission-based email perform better for both consumers and businesses. In 1999, we set out to solve the growing problem of email change of address by offering an Email Change of Address (ECOA) service modeled after the Post Office's National Change of Address (NCOA) system. Today, Return Path manages the largest consumer-reported email-change-of-address database, reconnecting more than 8 million customers with the companies with whom they wish to do business.

Our NetCreations division has a long history of consumer privacy and protection advocacy. We pioneered—and patented—the double opt-in email process, which ensures consumer control over their inbox and guarantees marketers that email messages will be welcome and generate a response.

Combined, more than 45,000 consumers and business professionals sign up every day for email services from Return Path. Consumer email privacy, permission and relevancy are the keystones of our business, creating many opportunities for marketers to connect with customers and prospects.

List Acquisition Solutions: When consumers and business professionals trust the source and the medium, your email prospecting will generate a higher response. Permission email is the most trusted form of digital marketing (Jupiter Research, 2004), and our double opt-in PostMasterDirect, SmallBizOwnersDirect and ITProsDirect files give you added confidence by identifying the best targets based on hundreds of interest categories. This industry-leading combination of permission and relevancy drives some of the highest response rates in the business.

Delivery Assurance Solutions: Your email must pass through a series of tests before reaching the inbox—blocking, filtering, blacklists and more. Return Path has pioneered deliverability solutions that combat false-spam problems for legitimate email marketers and raise all your response metrics—from inbox delivery to opens to clicks to conversion.

List Quality Solutions: Accurate lists are the key to email performance and deliverability, and nearly 40% of most marketing lists will degrade this year. Our

ECOA, email list hygiene and other services make sure you list is clean and growing.

Strategic Solutions: Make your email program extraordinary by tapping Return Path's industry-leading vault of best practices for optimizing response and building relationships. Our strategy team provides customized action plans that drive immediate results. Learn how to make your email more relevant, driving higher response while minimizing customer complaints.

Return Path helps more than 1,500 retailers and *Fortune* 1000 marketers improve their email lists and performance. Contact us at <u>rpinfo@returnpath.net</u> or visit the Sign Me Up! website at www.returnpath.biz/signmeup

About the Authors

Matt Blumberg, founder, CEO and chairman, Return Path

Prior to founding Return Path in 1999, Matt was general manager of the internet division of MovieFone, Inc., from its inception to the company's sale to AOL five years later, as well as vice president, marketing and product management, for the company's 777-FILM phone service. Matt has served as an associate with General Atlantic Partners, a private equity investment firm, and as a consultant with Mercer Management Consulting. He graduated from Princeton University. He is a frequent industry writer and speaker and is actively involved in boards and councils for the Direct Marketing Association and the Association for Interactive Marketing. He writes a blog about the email/online marketing industry, as well as leadership and management issues. It can be found at http://onlyonce.blogs.com

Michael Mayor, president, NetCreations

Michael Mayor is an eighteen-year veteran of the direct-marketing industry and a recognized pioneer of email marketing. Michael joined NetCreations as the company's third employee in 1998, and his vision and leadership played an integral role in helping it become the largest and most respected email list-management company in the industry today. Mayor is a leading advocate of privacy and speaks frequently at industry functions, including the FTC's Spam Forum on the Best Practices panel. He founded and currently chairs the Interactive Advertising Bureau's Email Committee and also writes a bimonthly column on email marketing for iMedia. Prior to joining NetCreations, Michael spent twelve years at Hearst Magazines.

Stephanie A. Miller, vice president, strategic services

With nearly twenty years of marketing, publishing and consulting experience, Stephanie has built and managed integrated direct-marketing programs for both business-to-consumer and business-to-business companies. An online marketing pioneer, she was the first publisher of the *Wall Street Journal Interactive Edition*. She held executive-level marketing positions with Hotmail and RealNetworks before working for six years as a marketing consultant in Silicon Valley, where, in addition to software, consumer and financial services clients, she worked with several email technology companies, including IronPort, MailShell, TeliVoice and MSN.

Tami Monahan Forman, director, strategic services

With her editorial experience and email business savvy, Tami helps Return Path clients establish best practices email programs, improve existing programs and build their businesses through email marketing. Prior to joining Return Path, she was the editor of News Corp's SmartSource.com, where she revamped their email newsletter and increased the open rates six fold. She also created the successful Coupon Alerts program—a new email format that saw open rates in excess of 20% and click-through rates of 70%. Before that she spent three years at iVillage.com, the web's premier site for women. In her role as food editor, she pulled a variety of levers—including email newsletters—to increase channel traffic by more than 200%.

0-595-33586-1

Printed in the United States
43625LVS00005B/134

9 780595 335862